NORWEGIAN CATCH-UP

To Maggi:

*Who rekindled my interest in both Norway
and economic development*

Norwegian Catch-Up
Development and Globalization before World War II

JONATHON W. MOSES
Norwegian University of Science and Technology
Trondheim, Norway

LONDON AND NEW YORK

First published 2005 by Ashgate Publishing

Reissued 2018 by Routledge
2 Park Square, Milton Park, Abingdon, Oxon, OX14 4RN
711 Third Avenue, New York, NY 10017, USA

Routledge is an imprint of the Taylor & Francis Group, an informa business

Publisher's Note
The publisher has gone to great lengths to ensure the quality of this reprint but
points out that some imperfections in the original copies may be apparent.

Disclaimer
The publisher has made every effort to trace copyright holders and welcomes
correspondence from those they have been unable to contact.

A Library of Congress record exists under LC control number: 2005005533

ISBN 13: 978-1-138-29616-9 (hbk)
ISBN 13: 978-1-315-10011-1 (ebk)

Contents

List of Figures

List of Tables

List of Abbreviations

C/L	Capital/Labor (ratio)
CPI	Consumer Price Index
DNA	*Det norske Arbeiderparti* [The Norwegian Labor Party]
GDP	Gross Domestic Product
GNP	Gross National Product
H-O-S	Heckscher-Ohlin-Samuelson
HP	Horse Power
IOM	International Organization for Migration
IWW	International Workers of the World
Kr	Kroner
kW	Kilowatt
LO	*Landsorganisasjonen* [Trade Union Organization]
NAF	*Norsk Arbeidsgiverforening* [Norwegian Employers' Organization]
NIC	Newly Industrialized Country
NKL	*Norges Kooperative Landsforening* [Norwegian National Union of Cooperatives]
ODA	Official Development Assistance
OECD	Organization for Economic Cooperation and Development
SCU	Scandinavian Currency Union
SSB	*Statistisk Sentralbyrå* [Norwegian Statistics Bureau]
TRIPS	Trade-Related aspects of Intellectual Property Rights
TRIMS	Trade-Related Investment Measures
WWI	World War One
WWII	World War Two
WPU	World Postal Union

Acknowledgements

About a decade ago, a colleague unwittingly introduced me to this book: Rune Skarstein asked if I might take over his annual lecture to an incoming group of foreign students—students that were attending our university on a scholarship provided by The Norwegian Agency for Development Cooperation (NORAD). The aim of this lecture was to introduce Norway's short, but remarkable, economic transformation to students from the developing world. These students came from every corner of the globe, and—when I got them, still early in their stay—were reeling from the shock of Norway's exorbitant cost of living. My task then, as now, was to explain how a country came to enjoy such remarkable wealth, from a position of such poverty, over such a short period of time. Norway's economic transformation is a wonderful story to tell, and I have looked forward to giving this lecture each and every year.

At the same time, Rune introduced me to a book written by Trond Bergh, Tore Hanisch, Even Lange and Helge Pharo, *Norge fra uland til iland* [*Norway from developing country to industrialized country*], which became a model for the book before you. Bergh et al. (1983) provided an easily accessible introduction to Norway's economic transformation—one that has influenced a generation of Norwegian students. This book had its own roots in an English version of a report published by the Norwegian Institute of International Affairs (NUPI).[1]

With a decade's experience of lectures behind me, and a good model textbook before me, I set out to plan a new book for foreign students of Norway's early economic transformation. Like Bergh et al., my objective has been to provide a user-friendly introduction to Norwegian economic history. In addition, however, I wanted to anchor that history in an updated and different international context. This, I hoped, would make the text more accessible to contemporary readers, allowing me to focus on external factors behind Norway's remarkable economic catch-up.

This ambition was not easy to reconcile with the demands of the modern publishing world. The market for English books on Norway is understandably small, and international publishers are reluctant to consider a book that could enjoy only a small print run. To overcome this reluctance, I was fortunate enough to receive support from the P.M. Røwdes Foundation and its chairman, Hans P. Struksnæs. Another central player in the origin of this book is the senior acquisitions' editor at Ashgate Publishers, Brendan George. Brendan provided much encouragement and useful commentary early in the project. Without the support of these two players, the book before you would have remained a pile of hand-scribbled lecture notes. To them both I am very grateful.

---

[1] Bergh et al. (1981) *Growth and Development: The Norwegian Experience 1830-1980* (NUPI/R 57, Norwegian Foreign Policy Studies 37, Oslo).

Most of this book was written while I lived in Dhaka, Bangladesh, where I enjoyed a leave of absence from my position in Trondheim. This has undoubtedly impacted the final product—but not in ways that may be immediately obvious. At the outset, my biggest concern was in obtaining necessary resources while sitting on the opposite side of the globe from my subject of study. Luckily, this worry proved unfounded. Electronic communications have made it remarkably easy to gain access to the background materials needed to write this book. There are an astonishing number and array of published articles and datasets available on the Internet, and e-mail makes it almost too easy to contact people that might provide extra help and assistance.

Rather, my experience in Bangladesh has made its impact felt on the book's tone. Being exposed to the harsh realities of Bangladeshi life has surely radicalized my approach and forced me to reflect more on the comparative lessons provided by the Norwegian experience. Economic development is a difficult and wrenching experience, and the study of economic underdevelopment is (and should be) driven by strong normative objectives. For a resident of the developed world living in Dhaka, every day is a reminder of the phenomenal and unjust differences that separate our life's chances from those offered to the average Bangladeshi.

In writing a book like this, any author must draw from a great many sources over a long period of time. I am no different in this regard, and my debts are many and widespread. Unfortunately, this is not immediately obvious from a glimpse at the book's bibliography. My desire for accessibility and readability has sometimes come at the expense of extensive referencing. As a result, there are many intellectual debts that I have incurred that do not appear in the bibliography.

I am also indebted to several economic historians who have forgiven my academic trespasses and helped me navigate the mostly deep, but sometimes turbulent, waters of Norwegian historiography. As a political economist by training, I have had little occasion to draw on my own research. Instead, I have relied mostly on a wide array of secondary sources and the guidance of friends and colleagues in the field of history. Among these, I would especially like to thank Hans Otto Frøland at NTNU's Department of History and Classical Studies for his insight and useful commentary at several junctures on the path to this book's completion. I am fortunate to work at a place that has such generous and helpful colleagues.

In addition, I owe two particular debts of gratitude to people who have shared the fruits of their own labor with me: John Moen at GraphicMaps.com for granting me permission to use their Map of Norway in Figure 3.1, and Camilla Brautaset for providing me with the data used in Figure 8.2.

Finally, the book before you has truly benefited from the input of several friends and colleagues who have helped by reading earlier drafts of this manuscript. In particular, I am sincerely thankful to Michael Alvarez, Maggi Brigham, Omano Edigheji, Stian Saur, and Indra de Soysa, as well as the publisher's anonymous reviewer, for their helpful comments. Despite all this generous help, the errors that remain can only be my own.

Chapter 1

A Cinderella Story

The history of Norwegian economic development is a Cinderella story.

At the turn of the 19th century, Norway was a poor, underdeveloped country on the margins of Europe: there were no banks, no institutions of higher learning, not even an indigenous daily newspaper. Indeed, Norway's infrastructure and level of development was so poor that Norwegian schoolchildren today are told that Bernt Anker, Norway's richest person at the time, sent his clothes to England to get them properly washed and starched. By the end of the 19th century, the conditions at home remained grim enough to encourage tens of thousands of Norwegians to emigrate each year.

Contrast this picture of Norway's gritty economic youth with the image of Norway as a mature economic power. At the dawn of the 21st century, Norway ranks consistently among or at the top of the United Nation's Human Development Index. In 2002, Norway was ranked first in the world on this index, followed by Sweden, Australia, Canada and the Netherlands. This index rates countries of the world in terms a composite scale that includes life expectancy, per capita income, educational enrollment and adult literacy. Beneath this aggregate index lies an unemployment record that has long been the envy of many, and a level of poverty that is hardly visible in Norway today.

As a small country, with less than five million inhabitants, Norwegians have come to expect that the outside world knows little about it. For the few that do recognize Norway as one of the richest and most developed countries of the world, the vast majority of these tend to explain Norway's wealth with reference to its North Sea petroleum reserves. These reserves were discovered in the 1960s, developed in the 1970s, and today feed an enormous investment fund managed by the Norwegian government. However, it is a mistake to think that Norway would be poor without oil: while oil is an important part of a story about how Norway rose from rags to riches, it is only the most recent chapter.

Norway's Cinderella story is much older than oil, and it can be told in two parts. The second part of this story is better known. Since World War II, the Norwegian economy has grown at a remarkable and steady rate: between 1946 and 1980 its Gross Domestic Product (GDP) grew by more than 350 per cent! Under the stewardship of the Norwegian Labor Party, this growth was engineered with active state involvement and economic management. Most impressively, Norwegians have engineered this growth while maintaining a vibrant rural constituency, a relatively egalitarian income distribution, and a wide array of public social services. In many ways, the Norwegian record in the second half of the 20th century is a model of social democratic economic management.[1]

While the social democratic chapters of the story are most familiar, they depend critically on an earlier, less known, part of Norwegian history. This story begins in the closing decades of the 19th century and tells of a poor country that manages the difficult transformation from a relatively static agricultural economy to a vibrant industrial economy. Over the stretch of a few short decades, the Norwegian economy (along with other economies in Scandinavia) outperformed the rest of what would become the OECD club, and probably the rest of the world. In effect, Norway was one of the world's first 'NICs' (Newly Industrialized Countries); a rare European tiger from the late 19th century. Most significantly, Norway's economic transformation occurred on an international stage that is not unlike our own: against the backdrop of liberalism and global integration. It is this story—of Norway's economic transformation in an era of globalization—I aim to tell with this book.

Motivations

There are at least three reasons why I believe that Norway's Cinderella story should be told now, a century later. Each of them, in different ways, concerns the ever-changing nature of the international context for economic development.

First of all, Norway's early economic development happened at a point in history that is remarkably similar to our own. The turn to the 20th century was a wondrous time of rapid technological changes, shrinking communication and transportation costs, and—as a result—an increasingly global marketplace for ideas, goods, services and factors of production. This was the first modern period of globalization, and countries that managed to develop in this context did so by both exploiting and heeding the opportunities and constraints imposed by globalization.

Although many students of economic development are enamored by the Norwegian social democratic example, and hope to learn from its institutional and political experiences, the heart of Norwegian social democracy developed in an international context that is radically different from our own. The postwar European economy was one that allowed for a great deal of trade protection in the reconstruction years. Domestic monetary and tax autonomy was secured in the details of the Bretton Woods' agreement that provided the institutional basis for what Gerard Ruggie (1982) called 'embedded liberalism'. In other words, the nature of the postwar international regime allowed states much more political influence in determining the character of their economic development.

Indeed, this postwar international system was a direct response to the perceived failures of liberalism during the interwar (1919-1939) period. As John M. Keynes was fond of explaining, signatories of the Bretton Woods agreement

---

[1] For a fuller description of Norwegian economic policy and growth over the postwar period, see Moses (2000).

aimed to exorcise the most frightening ghosts of the interwar period: devaluation, deflation and depression. More importantly, in the shadow of the Bolshevik revolution, these signatories realized the need for increased democratic accountability in economic management. If states could not provide more economic stability, with less unemployment and suffering, then they risked being overrun by a socialist revolution—either on the streets, or by the ballot box. This sort of democratic accountability for economic management could only be secured by allowing states some autonomy from international obligations. Thus, the postwar international economy allowed for economic sovereignty by way of limited trade protection and capital flows, fixed exchange rates, politicized central banks and extensive migration controls.

This sort of international environment no longer exists—although it may someday return in response to the excesses of contemporary liberalism. In this respect, the lessons of postwar Norwegian social democratic development are not particularly useful for students of development today. It is simply too difficult to limit capital mobility enough to allow economic managers the requisite control over the domestic economy. Social democracy depended on an autonomous tax base that is difficult, if not impossible, to sustain in a world where capital flees in search of the largest returns and the smallest tax burden. More importantly, social democracy relied on the state's ability to provide political, not economic, targets for the rate of social investment. To do this, the state needed to control the domestic capital supply (and with it, its price: the interest rate).

This brings me to the second motivation for writing a book on the Norwegian economic transformation in the late 19th century: to reflect on the complexities of globalization. In today's vernacular, 'globalization' has come to be understood as political impotency and the law of the jungle/market. As important venues in the world become increasingly integrated and dominated by large multinational actors (that include both multinational corporations as well as multinational and non-governmental organizations), it has become increasingly common to see globalization as a constraint on (if not a direct threat to) economic development and democracy. In the onslaught of liberal market forces, the state's modern armory of economic weaponry has proven frightfully ineffective.

But the previous era of globalization occurred at a time of remarkable democratic progress. The modern form of representative democracy was born during this era, and pressure to extend the democratic suffrage occurred hand-in-hand with expanding market interactions. This earlier period of globalization was not accompanied by political apathy. Quite the contrary! The modern socialist movement was at its most vibrant and powerful phase in these decades of free trade, investment and migration. As a consequence, the modern welfare state was born in an era of globalization, as workers fought for shorter working days and weeks, and greater social security.

Contrary to popular perception, there is no inherent reason to associate globalization with political apathy, democratic constraint, and the interests of big business. The social democratic state that eventually developed in Norway (and the international context in which it was embedded) can be understood as a direct response to the economic and political instability that was associated with a liberal world order. But the remarkable changes that occurred *during* the laissez faire period prior to World War I (WWI) suggest that the voice and influence of the little guy (workers, farmers and fishermen) was not insignificant.

This brings me to the third, and perhaps most speculative, motivation for writing this book. By implicitly contrasting the opportunities available to individuals during the previous era of globalization with those that exist today, we find that the nature of contemporary globalization is very different in one important respect: the lack of a migration option. While today's economy enjoys relatively similar levels of international trade and investment flows (compared to the early 20th century), national labor markets remain highly protected.

Before World War I, when conditions became intolerable, the poor and oppressed always had one last option: they could leave. This potential threat to exit provided an important impetus for policy-makers to consider the interests of workers, farmers and fishermen. Many states, including Norway, were forced to change their domestic political and economic landscape in order to stave off the potential migration outflow. Today's poor and oppressed do not enjoy this luxury (or influence).

By studying the effect of emigration on Norway's economic (and political) development during the first modern era of globalization, we can begin to draw a picture of the important influence that international migration had on economic and political development in Europe and the Americas. In particular, this earlier bout of globalization encouraged economic convergence and spread democracy among participating states. To the extent that modern globalization seems to lack these leveling effects, the absence of a migration option might be used to explain why globalization today appears antithetical to democracy.

When introduced in this way, these motivations implicitly suggest that I am proposing a model of economic development that is applicable for poor states in today's global economy—I am not. The economic gap that separated Norway from the world's richest countries in the 19th century was much smaller than the gap that today separates the world's richest and poorest countries and people. Indeed, a study done by Lant Pritchett (1997: 11) from the World Bank shows that the ratio between the incomes of the world's richest and poorest countries has increased from 8.7:1 in 1870, to 38.5:1 in 1960 to 45.2:1 in 1990![2] Thus, today's path from poverty to plenty appears much longer and more cumbersome than it did before World War I. Still, the Norwegian example is inspiring and informative in that it provides us with a glimpse of how the international context both limited and stimulated Norway's economic and political development.

History seldom repeats itself, and if it does—as Hegel reminded us—it often does so as farce. Interpreting Norwegian economic history in the late 19th and early 20th century does not provide a roadmap for developing countries with an eye for economic growth. My intent is much less ambitious and more honest: I

---

[2] This is a six-fold increase. In addition, Pritchett estimates that the standard deviation of (natural log) per capita incomes increased by between 60 and 100 per cent, and the average income gap between the richest and poorest countries grew almost nine-fold (from $1,500 to over $12,000) over the same period.

hope to present the historical evidence in such a way as to challenge the way we think about globalization and development at the beginning of the 21st century. It is only by thinking differently that we can move from where we are, to where we want to be.

The story line

These motivations help to explain the outside-in[3] perspective of the story that follows. In contrast to many influential economic histories in Norway—that focus largely on domestic factors for explaining Norway's economic growth (for example, demographic changes, technological adaptations and institutional developments)—this story focuses on international developments and how they affected Norwegian economic growth before World War I.

This perspective is not unique; indeed it is quite common to students of small open economies. After all, the Norwegian economy has always been too small to exploit economies of scale and/or to satisfy domestic demand. To survive, Norwegians depend on the international economy—as a source for their needs (food, investment, industrial inputs) and as a market for their own products and services. In this context, it makes sense to prioritize international developments for explaining Norwegian economic development. But, as we shall see in subsequent chapters, there are also good theoretical grounds for prioritizing international trade, investment and migration when explaining Norway's economic growth.

Before I begin a brief description of the chapters that follow, I should say something about the temporal parameters of this work. The empirical focus of this book concerns the period between 1865 and 1914. My objective is to capture the period of 19th century globalization, and Norway's response to changing global markets for goods, services, capital and labor. But history seldom accommodates simple temporal typologies—economic and political processes tend to straddle over the time frames imposed by academic observers. Such is the case in the chapters that follow. The processes that concern us have long trajectories. As a result, I sometimes follow a historical strand beyond these self-imposed parameters. After all, the economic and political ramifications of an invention, event, or an agreement can sometimes linger on for decades.

Given the outside-in perspective of the study that follows, it makes sense to begin by outlining the main characteristics of the international economy in the half century preceding World War I. In doing so, I provide the essential context for the remainder of the book and remind the reader of the similarities between this era and our own. Like our own time, the late 19th century was rocked by a series of technological, social and political revolutions that, in effect, shrunk the globe.

---

[3] 'Outside-in' is a reference to an approach in comparative politics that focuses on the way in which international events affect domestic policies, institutions and norms. It is akin to Peter Gourevitch's (1978) concept of the 'second image reversed'. 'Outside-in' approaches are usually contrasted against 'inside-out' approaches; the latter of which focus on how variances in domestic power constellations affect different international outcomes.

New developments in communication and transportation (for example, the telegraph and telephone, railroads, steel-hulled and steam-powered ships) made it both possible and viable to develop and exploit international contacts and markets. These technologies were supported with political agreements that facilitated economic exchange (for example, the demise of the Navigation Laws, the gold standard, an open migration regime), and a new Atlantic economy came into being.

Although my emphasis is on international factors behind Norwegian economic growth, I do not intend to ignore the domestic setting. For this reason, Chapter 3 provides a brief glimpse of Norway's institutional context at the turn of the 19th century. After several centuries under Danish rule, Norwegians found themselves under Swedish tutelage for most of the 19th century. This awkward relationship to its larger neighbors (and regional powers) had an enormous impact on the institutional and market structure that developed in Norway.

In Chapter 4 I will describe the main characteristics of Norwegian economic growth over the period, relative to other countries. This description elaborates on the role played by the three main motors of the Norwegian economy: farming, fishing and shipping. Although changes in these three sectors are all linked to international markets (links that will be developed in Chapter 5), their impact on Norwegian industrialization and subsequent economic development is so important that they deserve special attention. The key nexus for economic development is the delicate balance that modernizes primary production in such a way as to free up redundant (rural) labor for the nascent industrial sector, while maintaining productivity such that it can supply the needs of the industrial sector. This chapter illustrates how changes in the farming, fishing and shipping sectors affected demographic trends in Norway and abroad, laying the groundwork for major economic and political transformations.

In the following three chapters, five to seven, I take a specific international market and explore its links to Norwegian development. Each chapter begins with a very brief sketch of the economic theory that illuminates the growth effects of foreign trade, foreign direct investment and international migration. We begin with the most familiar territory: Norway's trade links to the outside world.

In Chapter 5 we examine the way in which changes in the international markets for grain, fish and shipping influenced Norwegian developments. Norway's reliance on these markets meant that it had to respond quickly and decisively to important changes internationally. The liberalization of European grain markets made it much easier (and cheaper) for Norwegians to import necessary foodstuffs. This allowed Norwegian farmers to switch from grain production to animal husbandry, freeing up much surplus labor in the process. Similarly, the liberalization of British shipping laws provided a new and bountiful market for foreign shipping companies, which Norwegians were well-placed to exploit because of their sea-faring history.

In Chapter 6 we examine Norway's reliance on international capital and investment sources. Until very recently, Norway has been a capital-poor country. Indeed, Norway's development prior to the 1870s is unique in the way in which collective arrangements were used to secure the capital needed to exploit new markets. Thus, local communities or producer networks often came together to finance a fishing or shipping exploit. As industrialization began to take hold, however, Norway became increasingly reliant on the import of foreign capital from across Scandinavia, the European continent, and from returning New World émigrés.

Chapter 7 describes the role of emigration in Norway's economic development. By the end of the 19th century, the economic and political conditions in Norway were so grim (or the draw of the New World was so strong), that Norway seemed to be suffering a demographic hemorrhage: only Ireland experienced a larger share of its population fleeing to the New World. While often ignored, this emigration had a substantial effect on Norway's economic development. As emigration eliminated much 'excess' labor, it increased the relative bargaining power (and wages) of the labor that remained behind. This provided important incentives for nascent Norwegian industry (and a transformed agricultural base) to employ labor-saving technologies. Returning émigrés brought with them capital, skills and habits from the New World that again boosted Norwegian productivity. Most importantly, perhaps, was the effect of emigration on the Norwegian political authorities: fearing an even larger outflow, local and national governments began to introduce reforms aimed at improving local conditions for potential emigrants.

In Chapter 8 I aim to tie these sundry aspects of Norway's economic development together to show how Norway relied on a complicated mix of factor and goods mobility to pull herself out of poverty. Norway's economic dilemma was to find a way to get rid of excess labor and to attract capital, knowledge and skills that could be used to spark its industrial transformation. Its access to world markets for labor, capital and goods provided Norway with just what was needed. What is all the more remarkable (seen from today's perspective) is that Norway's embrace of world markets did not seem to inhibit it from adopting and building strong democratic institutions and/or democratic controls on the domestic economy.

By the eve of World War I, Norway was approaching what would come to be called 'first world' economic and political conditions. The stage was set for Norway's social democratic transformation in the postwar period. But before that transformation could take place, the liberal order itself would be called into question, and a new, more interventionist regime would take its place. The seeds to this new regime were planted in the crisis years of the interwar period. The Norwegian seeds of change are examined briefly in an epilogue chapter that describes the nature of the Norwegian interwar crisis, and the important institutions and policies that were implemented to correct for the problems associated with liberal markets.

By the end of this story, Norway is ready to become a mature, developed economy. The trials and tribulations of her early economic development made a lasting impression on Norway's institutional landscape. As it turns out, this impression proved remarkably useful as Norway transformed itself yet again into a vibrant managed economy in the postwar period.

Norway's economic history is the story of a small country's transformation from rags to riches. The beginning chapters of this story describe one state's route to industrialization and the modernization of its agricultural production. It is important not to exaggerate the uniqueness of this story, as its general content is shared by several other neighboring Scandinavian states. This is a story about economic growth, accompanied by both hardship and opportunity, in a liberal and global economy. Perhaps the moral of this story is as important as its detail: Norway's economic break-through occurred in an international context of globalization. This is important to recall at a time when globalization seems to offer very little hope for developing countries.

But today's globalization is different in at least one important regard. International migration is no longer seen as an acceptable way to shrink the opportunity gap that exists between developed and developing countries. In this light, the nature of today's globalization seems relatively constrained and limited. While this story has hinted at the important role that emigration played in sparking economic and political development in Norway (and in Europe), we can only speculate about how increased migration might help today's poor and oppressed. Still, the lessons of history allow us an opportunity to speculate along these lines at a time when anti-immigration rhetoric in the developed world (and the walls that surround it) is approaching record heights.

By the end of the 20th century, Norway is again trying to re-make herself in a liberal image. Luckily for Norwegians, the trials of this transformation are less pressing, and the pain of transformation can be numbed with injections from Norway's enormous petroleum fund. As Norway again searches for her place in a world that has returned to a more liberal and global order (or, perhaps, disorder?), it behooves us to remember the remarkable role that she played in the last liberal order.

Chapter 2

Global Opportunities

Once upon a time...

Like all good stories, the story of Norway's Cinderella transformation begins in a far away time: a time that seems vaguely familiar, yet subtly different. After all, the late 19th century was filled with phenomenal changes and rapid developments. It was a time when the world reeled from the shock and excitement of new technologies that transformed production, transportation and communication. As a result of these changes, labor, capital and goods markets were increasingly exposed to international competition (and the challenges and opportunities posed by such markets) in ways that transformed them from national markets to truly international markets. This was an era of globalization, not unlike our own.

In pointing this out, I do not wish to engage the ongoing debate about whether today's world is more or less globalized than it was before World War I. For our purposes it is enough to recognize the transformative nature of new technologies and how they shaped world opportunities, without comparing them to our own world of change. Instead, this chapter aims to remind the reader of how interconnected the world economy was prior to World War I: a time when goods, services, capital and even labor were freely mobile internationally. In doing so, I loosen somewhat the temporal bounds of this project: many of the technical and organizational changes described below occurred early in the 19th century, but their effects were not truly felt until the latter half of the century. For example, the basic steam motor that transformed the world shipping industry in the late 19th century was already patented in 1769!

To describe this period of globalization, the chapter is divided into three sections. The first section introduces the remarkable technological changes of the time: changes in production techniques introduced higher levels of efficiency and optimism; while developments in modern transportation and communication effectively shrunk the world until it functioned like a single, world market for goods, capital, labor and services. The second section describes the development of these global markets in trade, finance and migration, as these are the main themes of three subsequent chapters in the book. Finally, I use the third section to briefly trace larger patterns of global economic integration over the entire period. With this global context as our backdrop, I intend to use the remainder of the book to show how Norway was able to exploit these global opportunities to escape from its poverty.

Globalizing technologies

As in our own time, new technologies in the late 19th century radically altered the nature of economic exchange and people's perceptions of time and space. The invention and spread of steam (and then internal combustion) power as well as mass production techniques transformed the way that goods were produced, raising productivity rates and standards of living, hand-in-hand. The rapid expansion of railway and shipping networks that exploited the new potential of steam and metal, shrunk the time, cost and hassle of international trade. Concomitant developments in the communication sector, such as the invention and spread of the telegraph (and later telephone) radically changed the way in which people communicated within and between countries.

Indeed, it is difficult to imagine the enthusiasm and optimism that these changes prompted. E. H. Carr (1961: 4) spoke of the way in which Britain was filled with the clear-eyed self-confidence of the late Victorian age. In the wake of one remarkable invention after the other, it seemed as though more progress was almost unimaginable. Indeed, it is often mentioned that the British commissioner of patents at the time had advised his government on the future necessity of closing the Patent Office, as there was apparently nothing significant left to invent!

While this naïve optimism seems utterly ridiculous now, one can understand the commissioner's exasperation by glancing at the chronology of significant technological developments in Table 2.1. This was a marvelous and exciting time of exploration, invention and discovery. For our purposes, the most important developments can be divided into three realms: production, communication and transportation.

Table 2.1   Chronology of technological developments

1807	Steamboat era begins as Robert Fulton tests his steamboat 'Clermont'
1817	Construction of Erie Canal begins
1819	First transatlantic steamship, the Savannah
1821	First electric motor
1831	Michael Faraday discovers electromagnetic induction
1837	Samuel Morse invents the telegraph
1844	Samuel Morse sends his famous first telegraph message, 'What hath God wrought'
1846	Suez Canal is begun
1851	First trans-Channel communication cable laid between Dover and Calais
1859	First trans-Atlantic communication cable laid
1860	Pony Express mail service begins between St. Joseph, Missouri and Sacramento, CA; Internal combustion engine
1861	Ernest Michaux invents the modern bicycle pedal and cranks
1869	Union-Pacific Railroad is opened; Suez Canal is officially opened
1870	First submarine; Northern Pacific Railroad begins

1873	Eliphalet Remington and Sons buys the patent rights to modern typewriter
1876	Alexander Graham Bell demonstrates his telephone
1877	Thomas Edison invents the first phonograph, microphone, and gramophone; First gas engine
1878	Electric light is introduced
1879	Thomas Edison invents the first filament lamp
1880	Construction work begins on the Panama Canal
1883	Northern Pacific Railroad is completed
1884	First motor car; First airship
1885	Karl Benz and Gottlieb Daimler build a single-cylinder car and patent a gasoline engine; First motorcycle is built
1888	George Eastman introduces Kodak camera
1893	Ford tests his gasoline-powered buggy in Detroit
1895	Guglielmo Marconi invents the wireless telegraph
1896	First radio
1898	Valdemar Poulsen invents the magnetic recording of sound
1900	Count Ferdinand von Zeppelin launches the first rigid airship
1904	Tans-Siberian railway completed
1913	Henry Ford installs the first conveyor belt-based assembly line in his car factory
1914	Panama Canal opened

A series of new developments and inventions radically changed the nature of production. These developments included new production technologies as well as new organizational forms. Most noteworthy was the invention of mechanical engines that came to replace the human, animal and water sources that powered previous generations. Already in 1769, James Watt patented a new design for the sort of steam engines that would come to transform late 19th century factories, ships and railways. In the early 1830s, Michael Faraday laid the groundwork for the development of modern electric motors, generators and transformers. The prototype of the modern internal combustion motor was developed in 1885 by Gottlieb Daimler, and by the First World War, Henry Ford had introduced a dramatically improved assembly line.

These new technologies and techniques revolutionized the nature and efficiency of world production and exchange. Like the goods they produced, news of these new power sources and techniques spread rapidly around the globe. Consequently, Norwegian production was also transformed, as described in Chapter 4 (although new ideas and technologies often took their time before reaching Norway's shore[1]).

---

[1] Norwegians frequently joke about the perceived lag between international developments and their adoption in Norway. When I first moved to Norway I was told a joke about an SAS flight from Stockholm (Sweden) to Oslo, Norway's capital city. As they began the plane's descent, the stewardess went on the intercom to announce to the passengers: 'We are now approaching Fornebu International Airport in Oslo. Please set your watches back ten years.'

Developments in the field of communication were perhaps even more revolutionary. The expansion of the modern postal service and the development of new technologies (such as the telegraph, telephone and radio) effectively shrunk the world to its inhabitants.

Tradition has it that one of the most influential postal reforms was inspired by Roland Hill's witness of a young village girl that had to reject a letter from her fiancé in London, because of the high cost of its postage. Hill offered to pay for the postage, but the girl refused with embarrassment. As it turns out, the girl and her beau had devised an ingenious system of letter-cover markings to signal affections without paying for the exorbitant postage.

Hill was so profoundly disturbed by this story that he initiated a campaign to reform the British postal system. When it was eventually passed into law in 1839, the reform introduced the idea of a fixed postage rate (a penny) to deliver any letter (under a given weight) anywhere in Great Britain.[2] Although the nascent postal system opposed the reform it was very popular with the public, and delivery rates rose precipitously. In 1839 the British postal service delivered just 82 million letters; in the year following the reform the figure more than doubled (169 million) and by 1850 they had delivered 347 million letters (Westergaard 1926: 32)!

The utility and accessibility of the post office grew across Europe and around the world. In 1874, a World Postal Union (WPU) was formed in Bern Switzerland among representatives of twenty-two (mostly European, plus the US) states. The union soon expanded to include British India, the French colonies, and—eventually—nearly every country in the world. In doing so, the Bern Treaty managed to unify a confusing international maze of postal services and regulations for the reciprocal exchange of letters. The barriers and frontiers that had impeded the free flow and growth of international mail had finally been pulled down. The utility and popularity of this is evidenced by the rapid growth in signatories over the next four years, when the WPU changed its name to the Universal Postal Union.

For many of us, the history of the US Postal Service *was* the Pony Express. In 1859, the existing US railroad and telegraph network did not stretch beyond the town of St. Joseph on the Missouri River. To get the mail quickly to California (two thousand miles away), the men of St. Joseph organized the Pony Express. Each day, with the arrival of a new train filled with mail from back East, a pony express carrier left St Joseph to cross the continent on a relay of horses, in ten to twelve days. Eventually, of course, the Pony Express was superseded by the telegraph, which stretched across the American continent to reach San Francisco in 1869, seven years ahead of the first transcontinental railroad.

The telegraph's history is often dated to May of 1844, when a forty-mile line of wire was stretched between Baltimore and Washington, enabling Samuel Morse to send his famous first telegraph message: 'WHAT HATH GOD WROUGHT!' Just six years later, in 1851, a trans-Channel cable was stretched

---

[2] Uniform postage rates, regardless of distance, were not introduced in the US until 1863.

between Dover and Calais, and a similar (albeit much longer) undersea cable was stretched between America and Europe in 1859—a link later extended to Argentina and Japan. The telegraph's novelty was superseded in 1876, when Alexander Graham Bell demonstrated his telephone. By the time that cabled connections were becoming commonplace, wireless (or radio) telegraphy was invented by a nineteen-year-old Italian boy, Guglielmo Marconi, in 1895.

These new communication technologies and organizations (such as the Universal Postal Union) tied people and markets together, in spite of the long distances that separated them. The trans-Atlantic telegraph cable facilitated flows of 'hot money' between London and New York, allowing traders on both sides of the Atlantic to keep abreast of market developments. Telephone and postal services helped entrepreneurs, traders and migrants to develop and maintain contacts and opportunities in foreign lands.

In Norway, this communications' revolution allowed exchanges to occur across a country that had always been handicapped by hard climate, a rugged terrain and a scattered population. Realizing the potential of these new technologies, the Norwegian authorities embraced them. In April of 1854, the Norwegian Parliament [*Stortinget*] authorized a new electric telegraph to be stretched between Oslo and Eidsvoll, while planning for an even broader network (to facilitate foreign trade and military contingencies). As elsewhere where these technologies were introduced, they proved themselves useful and popular. Communication networks spread rapidly with the new technologies. The Norwegian telegraph office [*Telegrafverket*], established in 1854, delivered 10.6 million telegrams in 1900, and 102 million in 1915. This is a ten fold increase in fifteen years! The national telephone company [*Rikstelefonen*], established in 1881, manually connected 1.4 million domestic calls in 1900 and eight million in 1915. Finally, the Norwegian postal service [*Postverket*][3] rode the same wave of popularity enjoyed by other national post offices, as the number of delivered letter increased from 58 million in 1900 to 127 million in 1915 (Hodne and Grytten 1992: 66).

Like the advances we saw in production technologies and in the field of communication, the transportation sector underwent a veritable revolution in the second half of the nineteenth century. Like the other globalizing technologies, these developments brought people and goods, from around the world, closer together. Better yet, the cost of world transportation and communication dropped sharply as a result, encouraging even more international exchange.

One of the most significant developments, and one tied closely to the expansion of the telegraph network (described above), was the expansion of national railway networks. To get an idea of how quickly railways were

---

[3] Although the Norwegian postal system can be dated to 1647, a new law in 1888 secured *Postverket*'s monopoly on the delivery of mail throughout the country.

expanding, we can compare developments on two continents over time. In 1850, Great Britain and Ireland had built some 10-11,000 kilometers of railway; just twenty years later (in 1870) the number had more than doubled to 25,000 kilometers! In the US, progress was even greater (understandably, given the distances to be covered). At mid century the US had laid about 14-15,000 kilometers worth of track, and by 1870 there were 85,000 kilometers on the ground. This contrasts with the 105,000 kilometers of track that stretched across all of Europe at the time (Westergaard 1926: 29).

New railways were connected across some of the greatest territorial expanses in the world. The first line across North America was completed in 1869, traversing 2,974 kilometers of mostly uninhabited terrain. Even longer was the Canadian Pacific Railway, at 4,677 kilometers, which was completed just a little while later. Both lines were dwarfed by the 1904 completion of the Siberian Railway (6,555 kilometers). Finally, in 1910 a transcontinental line was finished across South America: from Buenos Aires to Valparaiso, a distance of just 1,448 kilometers. In 1907, the world enjoyed about 968,516 kilometers of railway, excluding tramways. America enjoyed the longest lines, totaling 498,855 kilometers; followed by Europe (320,857); Asia (93,633); Africa (29,799); and Australia (28,592).[4]

Because of its rugged terrain, railway construction was a costly and difficult process in Norway, and these difficulties limited it impact on the general economy. In 1848 the Storting had already agreed to float a foreign loan to build a railroad network. Engineers, key workers and a good deal of material were brought from England, and the project was completed in just three years (1851-1854). In the 1870s, the original Eidsvoll railway was extended to reach Trondheim, and two additional links to Sweden were completed by 1880 (increasing the total network to more than 1,700 kilometers) (Derry 1973: 114, 128).

While the Norwegian railway effort would remain a relatively minor (if expensive) affair, a revolution in the shipping industry hit her much harder, and made a much larger dent. The details of Norway's tardy transformation from wood and sail to iron and steam is described in Chapter 3, so I will not dwell on it now. But it is important to recognize the revolution that these changes brought to world trade and migration. By adopting steel hulls and steam power, the shipping industry rapidly reduced the price (and increased the consistency and predictability) of long-distance freight. Before steam was applied to the propulsion of ships, the voyage from Great Britain to America was measured in weeks; at the beginning of the 20th century the time had been reduced to about six days, and in 1910 the fastest vessels could do it in four-and-a-half days. In the competitive environment of international shipping at the time, it is not surprising that the world trading fleet shifted rapidly over to steam.

Finally, a burgeoning network of canals and roadways were linking national and international markets in new and remarkable ways. A couple of

---

[4] The figures in this paragraph come from *Encyclopedia Britannica* (1911).

prominent Scottish engineers (Thomas Telford and John Loudon McAdam) developed new standards for modern road construction, and these standards spread quickly around the globe. These engineers designed a road foundation that was raised in the center (allowing water to drain off to either side) and they improved road-building methods by analyzing stone thickness, road traffic, road alignment and gradient slopes.

At the same time, monumental canal projects were being built around the world. In the United States, the Erie Canal was finished after the country's civil war. In 1869, the Suez Canal was completed and the journey from India to England was thus shortened significantly. Finally, the Panama Canal was officially opened on 15 August 1914.

A closer examination of the effects of the Suez Canal helps us understand how these new technologies fed off one another, as the Canal's completion encouraged the building of new steamships. At the time, Far Eastern trade was still dominated by sail. In the absence of sufficient coaling stations around the coast, steamers needed to carry too much coal to make the trip around Africa. The compound engine reduced fuel requirements, and the Suez Canal made it possible to pick up coal at Gibraltar, Malta and Port Said, in addition to shortening the trip from London to Bombay. Not only did the Suez Canal make it possible for steamships to compete on Asian routes, but the Canal itself was of no use to sailing ships: they needed to be towed for the roughly one-hundred mile journey.

In Norway, canal and road building were affected by the same sort of constraints that had lessened the impact of railroad construction. Although some of the main roads were designed by military engineers in the 1820s and 1830s, they were woefully inadequate in number and quality. Worse, the country's annual thaw played havoc on road construction. Thus, by the turn of the century, the total Norwegian road network was about 29,000 kilometers, but it was quite discontinuous, especially along the coast (Derry 1973: 113).

These new globalizing technologies provided the necessary infrastructure for a radical and global reorganization of world production and trade. Shipping, canals, railways and road networks made enormous contributions to national and international market integration in the late 19th century. World communication networks helped fuel and support these developments.

As a result, global markets for goods, services, finance and labor expanded throughout the century. Indeed, by the outbreak of World War I, world exports came to total 8.7 per cent of world output — and foreign direct investment had reached nine per cent of world output. Migrants flowed from the Old World into the New, in search of better opportunities. Trade, investment and migration were knitting the world ever closer, before the war tore it apart.

In subsequent chapters we will look at Norway's economic engagement with these international markets for goods, capital and labor. These chapters will show how Norway harnessed international opportunities and adapted to these growing markets. In short, Norway learned to develop and exploit its own comparative advantage. To better understand these opportunities, the following sections provide a brief description of developments in these global markets, beginning with the expansion of international trade in the late 19th century, followed by a description of international finance and currency markets, and ending with a short description of the burgeoning world market for international labor.

Trade

The spread of global trade was a consequence of the technological developments (and their effect on prices), described above, combined with a series of national and political developments most closely associated with Britain. This section will describe these political developments and their consequence for world trade.

On the political front, 19th century globalization begins mid century, and it begins in Britain. By virtue of its industrial lead in coal, iron, textiles, chemicals and machinery, Britain became the hub of the new world economy. Its pound acted as a reserve currency for international settlements and the Bank of England's discount rate became the standard followed by other national banks.

This is not to say that other states did not embrace free trade. Before 1860, a number of small countries (for example, Belgium, Denmark, the Netherlands, Portugal, Sweden and Switzerland) had already adopted liberal policy stances. But these countries represented just four per cent of Europe's population at the time (Bairoch 1993: 22). Norway, too, belongs to this group, as we shall see in Chapter 5. But Britain was undoubtedly the primary mover for greater international free trade.

To understand the expansion of free trade in Europe, we need to recognize that it consists of developments across two fronts concomitantly: one domestic, the other international. On the one hand, countries were developing more liberal and national markets at home. In already unified states, such as Britain, this meant standardization and regulation across the national market. In other areas, it meant the unification of once segregated markets.

While countries such as Britain and France had managed economic unification by the end of the 18th century, this process was still underway in Germany and Italy. Following the Congress of Vienna (1815), Germany was organized as a loose federation of 39 states, each economically independent. From 1819, a series of treaties was signed with other German states which culminated in the Prussian Customs Union, formed in 1831. Meanwhile, a similar union between Bavaria and Wurtemburg had led to the establishment of the Bavarian Customs Union in 1827. These two unions, together, formed the *Zollverein* in 1833 (effectively 1834), uniting 18 states and 23.5 million people in a common customs union. The emergence of a unified Italian state in 1861 had a similar effect on the growth of trade: generating new, larger, and more integrated markets.

These unified markets became increasingly liberal in their orientation, as best exemplified by the British case. In Britain, the crucial moves toward free trade already began in the 1840s. In his budget of 1842, Sir Robert Peel abolished the outstanding export duties on British manufactured goods, set aside her prohibitions on the export of machinery, and reduced the import duties on no fewer than 750 articles in the customs' list. Three years later, in 1845, Peel swept away an additional 520 customs duties and abolished the remaining export duties on raw materials. In 1846, the infamous Corn Laws were abolished (following the Irish famine of 1845-46), allowing Britain access to the cheap import of foreign corn. Finally, in 1849, the British Navigation Laws were repealed, allowing foreign carriers to transport British goods.

These British policies set the groundwork for further liberalization abroad. Although many of these policies were begun in the first half of the 19th century, their impact on the rest of Europe continued throughout the latter part of the century. As we shall see in subsequent chapters, Britain's repeal of her prohibition on the export of machinery, the fall of the Corn Laws, and the repeal of Navigation Laws all led directly to the growth of more internationally-oriented Norwegian production.

At the same time, the expansion of free trade relied on international developments such as the widespread adoption of free-trade policies and agreements. These policies reached a peak in the third quarter of the 19th century, marking the end of a system of privileged trading blocs and restricted commerce associated mostly with colonial empires. This expansion of liberal trade can be traced to a series of reciprocal trade agreements that began with the 1860 Cobden-Chevalier Treaty between Britain and France. These treaties included, among other things, a 'most favored nation' clause that fanned the spread of free trade like a wildfire across the European continent.

Over the next two decades, a network of similar treaties spread across Europe. France and Belgium signed a treaty in 1861; a Franco-Prussian treaty was signed in 1862; Italy entered the network of Cobden-Chevalier treaties in 1863; Switzerland in 1864; Sweden, Norway, Spain, the Netherlands and the Hanseatic towns in 1865; and Austria in 1866. By 1877, Germany had become (virtually) a free trade country (Bairoch 1989: 40-41).

Free trade and the resulting expansion in world commerce cleared the way for national specialization and a new international division of labor and resources. Population growth, international migration, gold discoveries, railways and the telegraph, extensive foreign lending and borrowing at low rates of interest—all of these things combined to provide a massive boost to international trade in the 1850s. As a result, small states like Norway could ride a wave of international opportunity, generated mostly by the actions of its larger neighbor states. As a consequence, Norway's poor factor endowments could be offset by the export of a few specialty goods, in exchange for a wide variety of inputs and consumer goods.

In per capita terms, world trade grew at a decennial rate of 33 per cent between 1800 and 1913; in the period 1840-1870 it reached a peak rate of growth of 53 per cent per decade (Hodne 1973: 97). The 1860s and 1870s were a golden era for free trade, and goods moved easily across borders. As late as 1879, an astonishing 95 per cent of Germany's imports were still free of duty. Low trade barriers led to an explosion of trade, so that US exports soared to seven per cent of its gross national product in the late 1900s.

Toward the end of the century, Europe returned to its protectionist ways. In 1875, Italy cancelled her existing trade agreements in order to adopt a more protectionist stance, and France attempted to do the same. Indeed, in 1878, France ended its agreement with England. In June of 1878, a new Austrian-Hungarian tariff policy was introduced that was protectionist in nature. The new German tariff law of 1879 was distinctively protectionist for such important goods as iron, textiles, corn, rye and oats. Only England continued to embrace free trade. As we shall see in Chapter 5, Norway attempted to stave off protectionism for as long as possible, but she too succumbed to protectionist pressure at the end of the century. All in all, however, it is important to emphasize that the level of effective protection in Europe remained low by 20th century standards.

Finance

A global financial system grew to support this expanding network of trade. This new system was home to a wide range of international borrowers and lenders, gathered in some of Europe's largest cities, to secure the capital for both private and public ventures. As was the case with the expansion of world trade, new and improved forms of communication and expanding colonial networks encouraged a nascent European banking system to penetrate and exploit markets around the world.

The sheer magnitude of these net international capital flows is impressive, even by contemporary standards. In 1914, Great Britain's net overseas assets were almost half of its total domestic wealth (47 per cent) or about 1.6 times a year's domestic product (Edelstein 1994: 173). While these markets provided capital for private ventures, states were also very active there, as they borrowed money to pay for both new (for example, the expansion of railway and telephone networks) and old (especially war) exploits. Indeed, by the end of the 19th century, net long-term international lending by major countries (relative to GDP) was about twice of what it is today.

Although lenders and borrowers began to act as part of a common (and connected) system of international finance, there were significant differences in the way in which the demand for national capital was met. In the United Kingdom and the United States, more (stock) market-oriented systems were developed, while France and Germany developed a bank-oriented system that provided longer-term credit needs. France's *Crédit Mobilier* (1852) became a model across Europe, especially in Germany, where joint credit banks such as *Dresdener Bank* (1870) and *Deutsche Bank* (1872) became extremely influential. Together, these European markets offered a plethora of investment goods for international borrowers, of both public and private persuasions.

To give you an idea of the interconnectivity and accessibility of these markets, we can look at them through the eyes of a contemporary investor. As John Maynard Keynes (1919: chapter one) noted:

> What an extraordinary episode in the economic progress of man that age was which came to an end in August, 1914! The greater part of the population, it is true, worked hard and lived at a low standard of comfort, yet, were, to all appearances, reasonably contented with this lot. But escape was possible, for any

man of capacity or character at all exceeding the average, into the middle and upper classes, for whom life offered, at a low cost and with the least trouble, conveniences, comforts, and amenities beyond the compass of the richest and most powerful monarchs of other ages. The inhabitant of London could order by telephone, sipping his morning tea in bed, the various products of the whole earth, in such quantity as he might see fit, and reasonably expect their early delivery upon his doorstep; he could at the same moment and by the same means adventure his wealth in the natural resources and new enterprises of any quarter of the world, and share, without exertion or even trouble, in their prospective fruits and advantages; or he could decide to couple the security of his fortunes with the good faith of the townspeople of any substantial municipality in any continent that fancy or information might recommend. He could secure, forthwith, if he wished it, cheap and comfortable means of transit to any country or climate without passport or other formality, could dispatch his servant to the neighboring office of a bank for such supply of the precious metals as might seem convenient, and could then proceed abroad to foreign quarters, without knowledge of their religion, language, or custom, bearing coined wealth upon his person, and would consider himself greatly aggrieved and much surprised at the least interference. But most important of all, he regarded this state of affairs as normal, certain, and permanent, except in the direction of further improvement, and any deviation from it as aberrant, scandalous, and avoidable. The projects and politics of militarism and imperialism, of racial and cultural rivalries, of monopolies, restrictions, and exclusion, which were to play the serpent to this paradise, were little more than the amusements of his daily newspaper, and appeared to exercise almost no influence at all on the ordinary course of social and economic life, the internationalization of which was nearly complete in practice.

As Keynes' quote attests, the pre-World War I investor sat before a remarkably diverse set of investment options. Indeed, an investment consultant of the time, Henry Lowenfeld, listed forty countries with stock markets open to British investors (1909: 49). Many of these markets were available by trading on the London Stock Exchange itself – either by purchasing stocks and shares in foreign firms listed in London, or by purchasing the securities of British firms with concessions to operate overseas.

As we shall see in Chapter 6, the Norwegian state and Norwegian industrialists came to rely heavily on these international sources of capital. Given its relative poverty and under-development, external sources of capital were necessary for Norway to modernize, and banks, markets and venture capitalists from across Europe's capitals came to her rescue (or came to take advantage of her precarious position, depending on your ideological persuasion).

International investors and borrowers were able and willing to come together because the values of their national currencies were linked to gold. This linkage eliminated exchange rate fluctuations among currencies, allowing traders and investors to discount an important source of risk. In short, investors and borrowers could be fairly certain that the cost of their exchange would not increase in the future because of changes in national exchange rates.

Indeed, the logic of the gold standard was (and remains) quite simple. Under such a system, paper money circulates as a medium of exchange, but it is convertible to gold on demand at a fixed rate. Thus, when several nations join in a gold standard, their rates of exchange (between national currencies) are effectively fixed. To be considered 'on' the gold standard, a country needed to meet two requirements. First, its central bank pledged to buy and sell gold (and only gold) freely at a fixed price in terms of the home currency. (For example, the Bank of England agreed to exchange a £100 pound note for 22 (troy) ounces of gold.) Second, a country's private residents could export or import gold freely. Together, these requirements provided the gold standard with an almost automatic mechanism for correcting a state's trade imbalances with the outside world.

This mechanism is based on the state's commitment to maintain gold convertibility, which restrains its capacity to create new credit (money). Thus, a country agrees to change its domestic supply of money in response to changes in its external account. To understand this linkage, consider the following, simple, example. If a country enjoys a trade surplus with the outside world (in other words, it exports more than it imports), and the payment for these exports is in gold, then the country in question would experience an increase in the amount of gold in its national coffers. This, in turn, would increase the domestic money supply, causing domestic (and its export) prices to rise. Thus, in the next round of international trade, the price of this country's exports would be too high, fewer people would buy them, and the country's trade balance with the outside world would correct itself. Of course, the same mechanism could allow states with a trade deficit to improve (read drop) the price of their exports (and subsequently improve their external balance).

Such is the way that the gold standard is said to have worked, in theory. In practice, of course, states managed to intervene and contravene its mechanical and automatic correction mechanisms. In addition, the gold standard itself was unable to provide sufficient flexibility in the world's supply of money, as the supply of newly mined gold was in no way related to the growing needs of the world economy. In addition, countries found it increasingly difficult to isolate their economies from depression or inflation in the rest of the world. Worse, the processes of adjustment for a country with a payments' deficit proved to be long and painful.

The gold standard period in history is often traced to the 1870s, although Britain had been using a de facto gold standard since 1717, when Sir Isaac Newton (then Master of the Mint) committed his serious accounting error.[5] Before the 1870s, most other countries in Europe were employing a bi-metallic standard

---

[5] Newton set too high a silver price of gold and drove all full-bodied English silver coins from circulation. As a result, only a few silver coins remained, most of them had become so worn that they were no longer profitable to melt and export; still, silver remained legal tender until 1774. After the Napoleonic Wars, England moved rapidly to a single-money system: in 1798 free coinage of silver was suspended; after 1819 silver could no longer be used to redeem circulating bank notes (paper could be redeemed in gold coin only); and, from 1819, England was on gold.

(using both silver and gold), but valiant attempts to stabilize the silver/gold exchange rate proved unsuccessful.

As a result, most of Europe jettisoned bimetallism (either one by one, or in groups) and linked to gold until the outbreak of World War I. In 1871, the new German empire adopted the gold mark as its monetary unit, discontinuing the free coinage and unlimited legal-tender powers of silver. In 1873, the Latin Monetary Union (France, Belgium, Switzerland and Italy) followed Germany's lead, and the US made a similar decision (the 'Crime of '73'). By 1878, silver had been demonetized in France as well as in most other European countries. Like domino blocks, world trading partners embraced gold, one after the other: Spain in 1876, Austria in 1879, Russia in 1893, Japan in 1897, India in 1898, the United States in 1900 (de jure), and so on.

Norway also joined this rush to link to gold by binding together in the Scandinavian Currency Union (SCU). Norway intended to join the SCU, along with Denmark and Sweden, when it was launched in December 1872, but found itself facing much domestic resistance. As in more recent times, Norwegians were then leery of any potential threat to national sovereignty. In April of 1875, the Storting passed a new law that committed Norway to the currency union (although the law did not take effect until 1 January 1877). According to the arrangements of the SCU, the national currency in each of these countries was accepted as legal tender in all three countries. Like most of the other gold standard and common currency arrangements of the time, there was a de facto end to the Scandinavian Currency Union with the outbreak of hostilities and the economic turmoil associated with World War I (while the de jure formalities of the SCU lasted until the early 1920s).

The late 19th century international financial system provided access to the capital necessary to fuel Europe's industrial transformation. It also provided the sort of system stability and predictability that could drive international trade and economic expansion. In short, free capital mobility and a stable system of international financial exchange provided the necessary fuel for a world economic machine that was producing at record capacity. Labor provided the other great input for this industrial machine, and it is to this international market that we now turn our attention.

Migration

Labor is the last, but not the least, of the great global markets in the late 19th century. The advent of cheaper communication and transportation technologies made it both feasible and attractive for millions of people to leave their homes and families in search of a better life abroad. The economic and political conditions that separated the Old and New World provided extra fuel for the fire. Finally, the absence of legal restrictions on mobility meant that national labor markets became just as globalized as did capital and goods' markets. Indeed, the amount of cross-national flows of labor is the most obvious and significant difference separating the nature of contemporary globalization and the globalization that preceded World War I.

One of the main reasons for this was that international travel at the time required little formal documentation and permission. Passports and visas were largely unnecessary, and those with enough money to pay for the trip (or a sponsor willing to cover the expenses) were free to escape the poverty and injustice of their homeland. Indeed, with the exception of just a few counties (for example, Japan), states did not place constraints on the movement of people across borders, except during periods of conflict.[6]

Actually, international norms were committed to the notion of free human mobility; as evidenced in the communiqués of various meetings of the Institute of International Law (for example, in Hamburg (1891), Geneva (1892) and Lausanne (1898)). Characteristically for the era, an International Emigration Conference in 1889 could declare:

> We affirm the right of the individual to the fundamental liberty accorded to him by every civilized nation to come and go and dispose of his person and his destinies as he pleases.[7]

These international norms were also reflected in national law. For example, immigration to the US was mostly unregulated before 1880: anyone who could afford the trip was let in (if not always welcomed). In the 1880s, racist campaigns in the United States led to the exclusion of Chinese and other Asian groups, but European and Latin American immigration remained unfettered until 1920 (Borjas 1990: 27). Even in the 'Old World', open immigration was becoming increasingly common. Thus, a German observer, Werner Bertelsmann, surveyed the changing political landscape on the eve of World War I:

> Because in recent times the position of foreigners has grown much different from before…most modern states have, with but a few exceptions, abolished their passport laws or at least neutralized them through non-enforcement… [Foreigners] are no longer viewed by states with suspicion and mistrust but rather, in recognition of the tremendous value that can be derived from trade and exchange, welcomed with open arms and, for this reason, hindrances are removed from their path to the greatest extent possible.[8]

---

[6] World War I (and the fear of foreigners that it generated) led the UK to impose a compulsory passport system in 1914 and this legislation was continued after the war; the US followed suit with an act in 1918, as did many other states. To arrive where we are now, states began to ratchet up migration controls with each conflict in the 20th century. As a result, international migration has become more and more narrowly defined in terms associated with the costs of war (in particular, refugee and asylum status), or (less legitimately) poverty.

[7] Cited in Thomas (1961: 9).

[8] Cited in Torpey (2000: 111).

Not only were there few legal impediments to international migration, but the sort of technological developments described at the beginning of this chapter facilitated greater migration. The price of travel decreased significantly during this period (mostly because of the rise of large shipping and railroad concerns), making it easier for the world's poor and displaced to move to new harbors of hope. A highly developed network of steamship and railway routes began to knit emigrant traffic from points of departure across Europe to their final destinations in the New World. The rise and spread of a world postal system, telegraphs and even telephones made it increasingly easier to get information about emigrant destinations, and to send word home of the immigrant's safe arrival.

Consider Kristian Hvidt's (1975: 194) depiction of the conditions that drove emigration from Denmark:

> Letters, money and prepaid tickets came in a constant stream, the volume of which would quite likely surprise most people, since the emigrants were generally believed to have formed the poorest part of the population and to have been characterized by intellectual narrowness and insufficient education. Improved economic conditions in the United Sates combined with the emotional longings inherent in emigration furthered both letter writing and sending tickets home. These personal contacts with the Old Country may well be sufficient explanation of why mass emigration accelerated whenever economic conditions permitted.

Hvidt's depiction highlights the last important incentive for international migration: economic gain. Economic conditions on both sides of the Atlantic functioned as a magnet for migration. By the closing decades of the 19th century, in the wake of the first great depression and a series of catastrophic harvests, there were enormous population flows crossing the Atlantic. The Irish exodus to the United States is perhaps the best known, but several European states experienced massive out-migration during this time.

This emigration was closely associated with the process and timing of industrialization in the sending countries. As Lydia Potts' (1990: 131-2) comparison of the timing of European emigration suggests, major waves of emigration took place immediately prior to the rise of industrialization in the sending countries. Thus, emigration peaked from Great Britain (1851), France (1851), Germany (1882), Holland (1882), Switzerland (1881) and Scandinavia (1882) prior to their respective industrial transformations. Only after the turn of the 20th century did Europe's late industrializers—such as Austria-Hungary (1907), Russia (1907), and Italy (1907)—begin to reach their peak emigration levels.

Under these conditions, it is estimated that over 50 million people left Europe for the Americas in the century following 1820 (Hatton and Williamson 1998: 7). But these immigrants arrived in waves over time; waves that carried with them different nationalities, and which corresponded to the arrival of their industrial revolutions at home. The rising trend of emigration to the US, in the form of growing waves, is clearly evidenced in Figure 2.1, before falling precipitously with the outbreak of World War I.

The United States tends to be seen as the magnet for most of the period's emigration, and it did attract a substantial number of immigrants, from Europe and elsewhere. But migration was extensive in other areas as well. The lack of legal restrictions and the falling price of transport and communication fueled migrations across Europe, east to Russia, from Asia to the new world, and to other places as well. Indeed, of the 15 million Italians who emigrated between 1876 and 1920, it is estimated that nearly half of these went to other European countries (Castles and Miller 1993: 53). Other countries on the geographic periphery of Europe, such as Poland and Ireland, also experienced significant emigration to other European states.

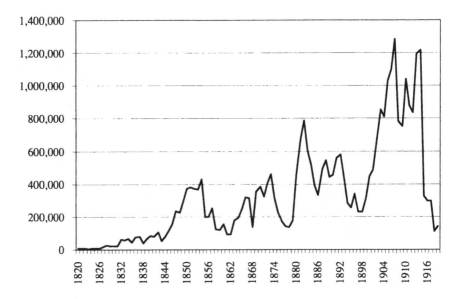

Figure 2.1   US immigration, 1820-1919

Source: OIS (2003: table 1)

In addition, other New World destinations attracted large numbers of immigrants. For example, the UN's International Organization for Migration (IOM) estimated that some 59 million people left Europe from 1846 to 1939, heading for the following (diverse) destinations: 38 million went to the US; seven million to Canada; another seven million went to Argentina; 4.6 million went to Brazil; and 2.5 million went to Australia, New Zealand and South Africa.[9] Worse, hundreds of thousands of indentured servants found themselves shipped to work in

---

[9] Cited in *New Internationalist* (2000).

the god-awful plantations and mines that littered Europe's colonies in Africa, Asia and Latin America.

As a result of these waves of migration to the New World, Timothy Hatton and Jeffrey Williamson (1998: 236) estimate that immigration may have augmented the New World's labor force by over 30 per cent. At the same time, immigration depleted the native labor force in the Old World countries on the periphery of Europe (for example, Denmark, Italy, Norway, Portugal, Spain and Sweden) by some 15 per cent.

Finally, it is important to note that a large number of these international immigrants eventually returned to their country of origin, bringing with them capital, new skills and norms, and access to foreign markets. Indeed, some migrant streams seem to be full of short-term laborers that migrated back and forth across the Atlantic following business cycles on both sides of the ocean. It is because of their frequent return trips that many Italian immigrants (who traveled between New York and Argentina at the turn of the century) were referred to as 'Italian swallows'. Indeed, it is common to estimate that some 30 per cent of the migrant stream at the time returned home. While his numbers seem phenomenally large, Charles Tilly (1978: 59) has suggested that the return rate in Norway and Sweden may have been as high as 40 to 50 per cent.

Global trends

The description above may give the impression that the global economy of this time can be characterized by one long, straight, march toward greater liberalization. This is not the impression I wish to make, as the liberal tide included several ebbs and flows across this period of time. In closing this chapter, I think it is useful to introduce Steven Krasner's (1976) characterization of these changes over time. While Krasner's periodization stretches beyond the narrower (temporal) frame of reference used in this study, and focuses mostly on trade, it offers a useful (and generalizeable) typology of the general trends in world markets before the Second World War.

In particular, Krasner (1976: 330) used three indicators (tariff levels, trade proportions and trade patterns) to divide this period into five distinct categories (the last two lie beyond our temporal framework). While the reference is to trade, the general characterization applies well to the period's capital and labor flows as well.

Period I: *(1820-1879)* This period was characterized by an increased openness: tariffs were generally lowered and trade proportions tended to increase. Although data are not available for trade patterns during this early period, Krasner notes the importance of recognizing that this increased openness is not a universal pattern. The US, in particular, is largely unaffected: its tariff levels remain high (and are in fact increased during the early 1860s) and American trade proportions remain almost constant.

Period II: *(1879-1900)* Krasner characterizes this period in terms of a modest retreat from liberalism: tariff levels tended to increase and trade proportions declined modestly for most states.

Period III: *(1900-1913)* Krasner characterizes this third period in terms of greater openness. Tariff levels remain generally unchanged and trade proportions increase for all major trading states (except the United States). Trading patterns became less regional in three out of the four cases for which data were available.

In short, world trade in goods, capital and labor ebbed and flowed throughout the period. The overall pattern, however, is one of increased liberalization until the outbreak of the First World War. This increased globalization of production and trade resulted in a phenomenal convergence in living standards across the Atlantic economy. Poor countries at the periphery of Europe tended to grow faster than rich countries at its center (or those in the New World). Between 1870 and 1913 there were powerful international forces at work: European labor migrated to the New World, and from low to high wage areas within Europe. Britain invested huge amounts overseas, while France and Germany invested large amounts in capital-scarce economies around Europe (for example, as we shall see, in Norway).

It is against this backdrop of world market trends that we can best see (and understand) Norway's remarkable economic catch-up. With this backdrop now in place, we can turn to the empirical matter at hand: the Norwegian experience.

Chapter 3

The Norwegian Context

The globalizing and integrating developments described in the previous chapter did not simply roll over the Norwegian economic landscape, transforming it into a cloned image of the British or the American economies. Globalization is a melding process, whereby international influences join with domestic institutions to produce hybrid mixtures. To understand the unique way that the Norwegian economy reacted to and channeled these global impulses, we need to begin by examining some of Norway's institutional history.

By institutions I do not mean to restrict the discussion to particular organizations, housed in brick and mortar. Like Douglass North (1990), I am referring to institutions in much broader terms: as the general rules and norms in a society (whereas organizations represent important players in that society). From this perspective, institutions help to determine the opportunities and constraints in a society: they allow us to overcome some of the uncertainties in human interaction. Thus, it is important to be aware of the role that history, culture and ideology play in framing human interactions. These underlying influences help us understand the nature and form of particular (formal) institutions and organizations as they develop in specific national contexts. Colonial states act differently than superpowers; states that rely on the extraction of natural resources act differently than industrial producers; small states act differently than large states; and so on. The reasons behind these sundry actions are complicated, but they should not be ignored.

Norway's institutional context is marked by three important and interrelated characteristics. First, Norway has been blessed by geography, and the first part of this chapter provides a brief introduction: it is a country rich in natural resources that are scattered in such a way that has hampered economic and political concentrations of power. Natural resource extraction is so central to the Norwegian story that much of the next chapter is devoted to describing the central role played by fishing, farming and shipping. Second, the Norwegian state is very young; before 1905 Norway found itself under the tutelage of either Sweden or Denmark, and it has inherited much institutional baggage from these relations. For this reason, the second part of this chapter will trace Norway's political history over a longer period in order to illustrate the nature of these foreign ties. Finally, and as a result of these external ties, Norway's institutional landscape was late and slow in developing. The third section of this chapter describes these nascent economic and political institutions. By the eve of World War I it is possible to trace the outlines of a Norwegian model that rests on an increasingly active engagement of the state in economic affairs and (relatedly) a growing and radicalized labor movement.   Despite this evident trend, the period under consideration was largely untouched by the labor movement that we traditionally associate with Norwegian economic development.

This chapter is an ambitious one in that it provides a great deal of background information that I hope to draw from in the chapters that follow. As a consequence, in the first two sections I relax the temporal bounds of this study significantly. This allows us to trace the deeper institutional roots to Norwegian economic success in the late 19th and early 20th centuries. Then, in the third section, I focus the reader's attention on Norway's institutional landscape in the four decades prior to World War I. As this section covers a great deal of very important terrain, it is longer than the first two sections. I hope that both the broad and the narrow temporal surveys will help the reader better understand the domestic institutional determinants of Norwegian economic growth during this period.

Geography

To understand Norwegians one has to come to grips with the landscape and climate in which they live. Norway consists mostly of a chain of mountains that forms the backbone of the Scandinavian Peninsula.   As shown in Figure 3.1, Norway stretches to 71 degrees North, and a third of Norway climbs above the Artic Circle: occupying the same cold part of the globe as Greenland, Siberia and Alaska. Not only is Norway located very far to the North; it is long—stretching over thirteen degrees of latitude.   To comprehend Norway's length, consider the following thought experiment: imagine a map of Europe stretching from Northern Norway to the Mediterranean. If we could cut out Norway from this map, and pivot her on an imaginary axis at its southernmost point, northern Norway would swing all the way down to Rome!

In addition to being a very long and mountainous country in Northern Europe, Norway's most distinguishing geographic characteristic is its meandering coastline.   This combination of mountainous terrain, dense forests, and deep-cutting fjords encouraged the dispersion of coastal communities that relied almost entirely on costal navigation to communicate.

Although a significant chunk of Norway lies above the Artic Circle, the climate is milder than expected, given its location. This is a result of Norway being warmed by a Gulf Stream that channels warm air and water from the Gulf of Mexico to the western part of the country. This relative warmth provides excellent conditions for the proliferation of wildlife—both onshore and off.

After a long hiatus, economists have recently returned to the role of geography in explaining and understanding economic development. In particular, new work is examining the roles played by such diverse geographic attributes as soils, river navigability, whether a country is landlocked, ecozones, population densities, disease vectors, and so on, in explaining different development outcomes around the world.[1]

Figure 3.1   Map of Norway

Map provided by: www.worldatlas.com

---

[1] Harvard University's Center for International Development has played an important role in this rebirth (see http://www.cid.harvard.edu/cidglobal/economic.htm). For an influential paper on the general relationship between geography and economic development, see Gallup and Sachs (1999).

In this context, it should not be controversial to suggest that Norway's unique combination of geology and climate has influenced its social and economic development over the years. As only three percent of Norwegian territory is arable, it was not possible to establish large concentrations of land-based authority throughout most of the country. For this reason, Norway escaped many of the feudal relationships that came to dominate in Europe. Indeed, the absence of an aristocracy and the proliferation of small, independent peasants and fishermen combined to make Norway an unusually egalitarian country (although hers was an equality of poverty).

Without larger farms and the specialization that it often encourages, Norwegian peasants survived by combining trades in ways that best exploited Norway's natural landscape and resources. In short, Norwegian peasants combined farming, fishing, hunting and foresting to eke out a meager living in the shadows of her mountainous fjords.

While living off the land was necessary for survival, natural resource extraction was also the source of Norway's comparative advantage. Indeed, this survival strategy can be traced back to the Viking Age (about 800-1050), when Viking wanderlust is often explained in terms of an abundance of able-bodied seamen and a shortage of arable land. What began largely as marauding expeditions to the British Isles, became — over time — a permanent effort to establish Norse settlements across the North Atlantic. For better or for worse, Europe (and beyond?!) became intimately familiar with the superiority of Norwegian boat-building and sea-faring traditions, and their insatiable appetite for new land.

Political history

It was these geographic and early political attributes that made Norway an attractive target for larger regional powers to the east and south. The relatively small and thinly-spread powerbase of the Norwegian aristocracy was little match for their Swedish and Danish counterparts. Small to begin with, the Black Death had decimated the Norwegian population (including its aristocracy) — reducing it by half, or possibly a third, of its pre-1350 population. Shrinking revenue bases prompted the king and nobility to extend their tax bases across national boundaries. Political unification was spread by economic necessity and consummated by inter-Scandinavian royal marriages.

In 1389 the three Scandinavian kingdoms were united. Just a couple years earlier, the Norwegian royal blood line had died out (with Olav IV), prompting the Norwegian Council of the Realm to elect Erik of Pomerania as their king. Because of Erik's young age, his grand aunt (Margrethe) was appointed Regent — and it is she that united Norway, Sweden, and Denmark in the 'Union of Kalmar'. Margrethe's scheming managed to bring an end to Norwegian independence for some 500 years. Unfortunately (for Norwegians), things were to get worse before they got better. In 1536, Denmark's King Christian III made Norway fully subservient to the Danish Crown: formally disbanding the Norwegian Council and undermining the autonomy of the Norwegian Church. From 1660, a new constitution provided the Danish monarch with absolute powers over both kingdoms so that Denmark and Norway were increasingly treated as a single economic and political unit.

From their position of power, Danes came to control Norwegian political, cultural and economic production. Most of the country's management and trading activities were located in Copenhagen and the state played an important role in developing Norwegian natural resources. In the 17th century, the Danish monarch (Christian IV) established a number of trading companies and encouraged the factory-like production of textiles in Norway; he was also responsible for establishing some of Norway's most important mines (for example, silver in Kongsberg and copper in Røros). Later, in 1737, Denmark was accorded sole rights to the sale of grain in southeast Norway and was granted a corresponding monopoly on the sale of iron from Norway.

More importantly, perhaps, was the important role that the Danish state played in providing a legal, regulatory, and market infrastructure that further facilitated trade in (and with) Norway. Danish investment capital, trading monopolies, and trade networks effectively turned the Norwegian economy into a raw-materials supplier for Denmark. While this relationship implied dependency on the part of Norwegian suppliers, it also provided a great deal of capital, expertise and access that came to benefit the local economy. After all, it was under Danish rule that the Norwegian export markets for fish, timber and mining products (not to mention a nascent domestic shipping industry) were developed.[2]

Obviously, Norway's dependency on Denmark affected the character of Norwegian economic growth. Norway became increasingly reliant on the production and export of raw materials (for example, timber, fish and metals). In return, Norway came to depend more and more on Danish imports across a variety of sectors, including agriculture, manufacturing and culture (for example, books, priests and jurists).

As one might expect, this increasing dependence on Denmark proved to be problematic when nationalism began its march across Europe. By the end of the 18th century, the roots of a nascent nationalist movement in Norway were beginning to take hold. Perhaps the clearest symbol of this is the creation of the Royal Norwegian Society for Development [*Selskapet for Norges Vel*] in 1809, which lobbied extensively for the creation of a Norwegian university. At about the same time, Norwegian timber merchants began to complain about the lack of a national (Norwegian) bank. Over time, these two demands came to symbolize a growing nationalist consciousness in Norway, and the Danish crown eventually (if reluctantly) succumbed to pressure to establish both.

In 1811, King Frederik VI authorized a national Norwegian University in Oslo. When one considers that the first university in Sweden was established at

---

[2] This is not to ignore the deeper roots of the Norwegian fish and timber trade—roots that can be traced all the way back to the Hanseatic League of the 13th, 14th and 15th centuries, when Norwegian fish (and later timber) exports were plied to a broad alliance of trading cities.

Uppsala in 1477, and its Danish counterpart at Copenhagen began in 1479, the University of Oslo was over three centuries late in coming. This tardiness can be interpreted as a symbol of Norwegian backwardness at the time. When it was opened in 1813 (as The Royal Frederik University!), the conditions in Oslo were relatively meager: classes where held in rented buildings for 17 students and six teachers. Still, this was a start; by the middle of the 19th century the University finally had its own building complex (on Oslo's main boulevard, Karl Johans gate—then Slotsveien).

The pressure for a domestic banking industry was satisfied at about the same time: in 1816 Norway's central bank [*Norges Bank*] was established. In the early years, Norges Bank functioned as the most important provider of domestic credit (indeed, Norway did not get its first savings' bank until 1822 and its first business bank until 1848). Equally important was the role Norges Bank played in securing a stable value for the Norwegian currency. This is no easy task, even for established central banks, but Norges Bank finally managed to secure a stable and convertible currency by 1842. While the intervening years were filled with mistakes and the pains of maturation, the subsequent years can be characterized by an economic predictability and stability that encouraged economic growth. These developments will be examined in greater detail in Chapter 6.

In 1814, Denmark's proprietary over Norway ended abruptly. As an ally of Napoleon, Denmark found itself holding the short end of the stick as the hostilities in Europe came to a close. When France attacked Russia in 1812, Sweden joined Russia to repel the French invasion. As a reward for their assistance, Sweden was promised Norway as booty. With Napoleon's (1813) defeat in Leipzig, the Swedish king (Carl Johan) led an army against Denmark, forcing the peace agreement that secured him Norway.

For the next ninety-one years, Norway found itself uncomfortably under Swedish rule. In many respects, however, this rule was more de-jure than de-facto. In one of those delightful quirks of history, Norwegians managed to convene a constitutional assembly in Eidsvoll and declare independence during the commotion that surrounded the cessation of European hostilities in 1814. Indeed, it is the signing of this constitution (on 17 May 1814), rather than their eventual independence from Sweden in 1905, that is celebrated as Norway's national holiday. For most Norwegians, 1814—not 1905—signals the birth of an independent Norwegian state.

Nevertheless, with the fourteenth paragraph in the Treaty of Kiel, Carl Johan absconded with Norway from the defeated King of Denmark. Although Norway was proclaimed a kingdom in its own right; it was formally unified with Sweden. In practice, Norwegians secured a remarkable degree of political autonomy: they were given control over taxation, legislation, expenditures—even the right to raise a national defense force. Full independence, however, was not within grasp, as Norway was denied the right to its own representation abroad.

Over the intervening years, until full independence in 1905, the Norwegian polity grew in tact with the pace of developments in Europe. The new constitution of 1814 was the most democratic system of representation in Europe: all freeholder peasants and most lease-holders were given the right to vote. In practice, however, the government continued to be in the hands of a small elite group of officials and patricians: universal male suffrage was not obtained until 1898, and women did not secure the vote until 1913. Still, the 1814 constitution was a remarkably democratic document for its time: it was a bourgeois, constitutional, law-based *rechtsstaat* (a government by laws, not men), with few constraints on commerce/business. Its ideology and political content cover familiar territory: borrowing from Rousseau's concept of popular sovereignty, Montesquieu's separation of powers, and a broad liberalism that is reminiscent of John Locke.

Throughout the period of Swedish tutelage, Norway continued to refine its system of democratic representation. Most significantly, Norway witnessed a social, cultural and religious mobilization that activated the peasantry and propelled it onto the political landscape. Peasants organized themselves and established alliances with town-dwellers (artisans, teachers, lawyers, and such) in opposition to the central administrative elites. This alliance soon gained control of the Storting—and launched a long series of attacks that resulted in a political bifurcation between two main political movements: the Liberal or Left [*Venstre*] represented an alliance of rural populists and urban radicals that won overwhelming victories at the polls in 1879 and 1882, while the Conservative or Right [*Høyre*] rose in opposition to the perceived attack on Norway's young constitution. The changing landscape of Norway's nascent political parties is depicted in Figure 3.2 below.

In 1882-85, Venstre dominated the political landscape—securing over 80 per cent of the seats in Parliament. By contrast, Høyre never secured more than 51 per cent of the seats during the period under consideration. Compared to these two largest parties, however, the parliamentary influence of a fledgling Labor Party was not evident until after the turn of the century. By 1912, the Labor Party managed to secure 23 per cent of the seats—slightly more than Høyre, but less than half of the number of seats won by Venstre.

The political struggle between Venstre and Høyre was messy, and the country was brought to the verge of civil war at least two times. In 1884, however, these struggles came to an abrupt end as the parliament introduced a series of dramatic impeachment proceedings against the King's Council. The Liberals used their parliamentary majority to pack the Court of Impeachment, guaranteeing a politically-acceptable verdict. The only remaining uncertainty lay in the King's response. In the end, the King took the safe route in asking the Liberal Party leaders to form the cabinet—formally establishing parliamentarism in Norway. Thus, while there would be a number of subsequent changes to the electoral laws, the basic framework for a democratic state had been established by the mid 1880s.

By the end of the 19th century, Norway was developing its own political institutions of sovereignty: institutions that captured and broadcast a growing voice for farmers, fishermen and workers. Over time, this democratizing influence would introduce important changes in terms of liberalizing the domestic (and

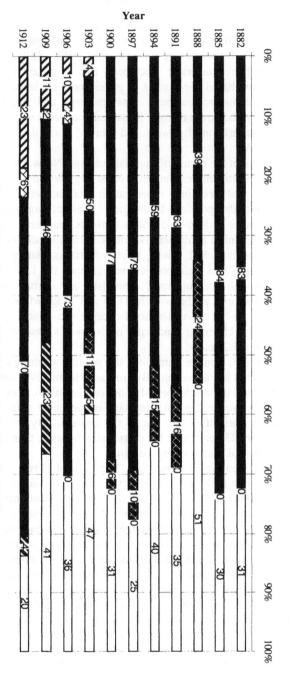

Number of Seats in Parliament

0%　10%　20%　30%　40%　50%　60%　70%　80%　90%　100%

1882
1885
1888
1891
1894
1897
1900
1903
1906
1909
1912

Year

◩ Labor　◪ Labor Democrats　■ Left　◪ Moderate Left　◩ Liberal Left　□ Right

Figure 3.2　Balance of political power, 1882-1912

Source: Nerbøvik (1999: 227)

international) regime for trade and exchange. In other words, elite privileges were increasingly difficult to maintain in the new democratic environment.

At the same time, Norway's relationship to Sweden (like its earlier relationship to Denmark), was having a significant impact on the nature of Norwegian economic development at the time. As we shall see in Chapter 5, joining forces with Sweden instantaneously tripled the size of the Norwegian home market. By 1815, customs tariffs on grain, fish and foodstuffs to Sweden had already been reduced (by 50 per cent if transported by sea; without duties, if transported by land). In 1827, Norwegian ships were given free access to Swedish harbors and could carry Swedish goods unhindered by Sweden's navigation laws. Finally, a full free trade area with Sweden was created in 1874, when virtually all trade barriers between the two countries were removed. Indeed, when Sweden moved to restrict free trade (in 1888), Norway stayed committed to a free trade policy — and, in doing so, was able to undermine Swedish producers in the common market. Eventually, Norway's commitment to free trade proved too costly for Sweden, and she annulled the free trade area by introducing custom dues on Norwegian goods in 1897.

The Norwegian system

This brief overview of Norwegian history has brought us to the temporal threshold of this study: circa 1865. In it we have learned that the Norwegian economy was heavily influenced by its unique geographic qualities and its political ties with its neighbors: there was little domestic concentration of political and economic power, the economy relied heavily on natural resource extraction and trade, and the general institutional landscape was strongly influenced by its dependent relationship to (especially) Denmark. By the middle of the 19th century it is possible to detect several important national institutions (for example, the central bank, a national university, and a democratic parliament) that would significantly influence future economic developments.

If Norway's natural resources can be used to explain the character of her pre-industrial economy, they can also be used to explain its tardy entry into the ranks of industrialized countries. Norway lacked access to coal, iron-ore and capital: *the* central inputs to early industrialization. Her fledgling industries continued to rely on the waterwheel, as Britain and the leading industrial economies were rapidly transforming to a coal-based industrial footing. The growth of Norwegian iron foundries was constrained by the need to import coke-made iron from England, as Norway's traditional (charcoal-based) iron was less attractive in international markets. Finally, and as we will examine more closely in a subsequent chapter, Norwegians needed access to new and alternative sources of finance as the 19th century came to a close. Hence, Norwegian industrialization was both late and slow in coming. As a result, the Norwegian population remained largely rural: by the mid 1800s, only about one eighth of the population was town-dwellers (compared to about half the population of England at the same time).

The 19th century was the domain of liberalism, and liberal thought made strong inroads to Norway following Danish rule. The 19th and early 20th centuries were pitted with new laws that dismantled privileges and allowed enterprise, capital and people greater freedom of movement. Industry and commerce benefited from a relatively low level of taxation (direct state taxes had been abolished in 1838), while new customs and treaty agreements allowed Norwegians to exploit their international comparative advantage in a few key areas.

It is in this wider ideological context, characterized by greater international exchange and liberalism, that we should interpret some of the more unique characteristics of the Norwegian approach to economic development. Despite strong liberal tendencies in the young Norwegian constitution, the Norwegian state took on an increasingly active role in supporting and encouraging the sort of modern infrastructure that could facilitate trade. Already in 1845, the government had established a Ministry of the Interior under Frederik Stang, which had responsibility for supervising the expansion of road, shipping, railway and communication networks. The state's active involvement was, in part, justified with reference to the handicaps of climate and geography; it was argued that these constraints made it difficult (and expensive) for private enterprise to build a modern communication network in Norway.

As government involvement increased, a new hybrid political constellation came into being—one which A. M. Schweigaard referred to as 'the Norwegian system'. In an 1868 speech to parliament, Schweigaard contrasted the Norwegian government's (successful) activity as a mortgage banker with the less favorable experiences in Sweden with private banking activity.[3] Under this new Norwegian system, the central authorities were able to use their superior credit-rating to obtain capital from abroad, and supply technical supervision and general oversight over larger investment projects. This dependence on foreign capital, and the government's role in securing it, will be described in Chapter 6.

For now, we might focus our attention on the role of the state in another influential arena: the development of Norway's concession laws. From 1888, all foreigners (except Swedes) were required to secure permission to own real property in Norway. At first the law was not followed in practice—as so much of Norway's natural resource extraction relied on foreign initiative, skill and capital. But as foreign interests became more and more dominant, and as Norwegian nationalism grew, so too did pressure to maintain some sort of political control over domestic natural resources.

By 1906, this pressure could not be contained any longer. At the time, three quarters of Norway's largest hydroelectric installations were already owned by foreigners. Indeed, new developments in the field of electrochemistry suggested that world demand for Norwegian hydroelectric power would only grow.[4] Worse, there was a common concern that simple (parochial) Norwegians

---

[3] Speech of 7 November 1868: *Stortings-Tidende*, 1868-9, Storting, 45.

[4] In particular, Sam Eyde and Kristian Birkeland developed a means for manufacturing artificial nitrates from atmospheric nitrogen by means of (relatively cheap) hydroelectric

could not defend their interests in the face of large international concerns. This perception of Norwegian incompetence was strengthened by the fact that half of the Rjukan power station (at the time, the world's largest) had been sold for just 600 kroner!

In April 1906, the so-called Panic Law was passed to satisfy the sense of outraged nationalism that was sweeping across Norway. This law imposed a temporary ban on the foreign purchase of Norwegian waterfalls (or the purchase by limited companies that might conceal foreign interests), but the government could offer concessions to this law, as it saw fit. Two months later, this ban was extended to cover forest and mining properties, and required that any company receiving a concession must have its seat of management in Norway. By 1907, the hiring out of hydroelectric power was brought completely under public control.

In effect, the concession laws prevented all private interests (of both Norwegian and foreign background) from acquiring land, forest and water rights. In their final form, these laws allowed the state to gain compensation for foreign ownership and control over common natural resources. But this concession was only granted for a limited period of time (between 60 and 80 years). After that time, ownership was returned to the state, free of charge.

It is hard to exaggerate the influence that these concession laws had on subsequent developments—developments that stretch far into the postwar (WWII) period. Arguably, these regulations stimulated the Norwegian economy and lightened the burdens of local authorities. When the concessions eventually expired, they secured enormous assets for the state—as these resources became public property. More importantly, the laws required the use of Norwegian workers and materials, and obliged foreign firms to encourage and support infant domestic industries. When oil was eventually discovered off the Norwegian coast in the post World War II period, these same laws were used to secure a central position for Norwegian firms until they became strong enough to fend off international competitors.

This encouragement for domestic import substitution extended beyond those areas of the economy that were formally governed by the concession laws. From our contemporary vantage point, one of the most impressive characteristics of early Norwegian economic development is the degree to which it was possible for Norwegian entrepreneurs to re-engineer and reproduce foreign technologies for the domestic market. Norwegian firms first gained access to industrial technologies by importing foreign goods; they then imported foreign craftsmen (to repair and re-engineer these products for the Norwegian markets). The third stage in this informal process of industrial domestication was to train a generation of Norwegian craftsmen and entrepreneurs to copy foreign technologies. In effect, local markets, regulations and patenting restrictions allowed domestic producers a protective niche within which they could develop new skills, technologies and markets.

---

power. Their work eventually led to the formation of *Norsk Hydro*, one of Norway's most influential firms in the postwar period. See Chapter 4.

As elsewhere in Europe, the Norwegian state was active in coordinating and spreading public education. While the first education law in Norway can be traced back to a Danish law of 1731, it was not until 1827 before all Norwegian children between the ages of seven and fourteen were guaranteed a general education. Still, recent local studies have revealed evidence of a remarkably literate peasant population in the 18th century. By the 1870s, the Norwegian public school system underwent a number of improvements under the leadership of headmaster and parliamentarian, Johannes Steen. In particular, the urban monopoly on secondary education was undermined, as an intermediate school level was introduced to fill the gap between elementary education and matriculation at the gymnasium. At the same time, a Danish Folk High School system was introduced—offering an attractive opportunity for the rural student (as it was based mainly on residential courses for a few months' duration). By 1889, a Public School Law was passed, depriving bishops and parish clergy of their traditional influence over elementary schools.

Table 3.1   School enrollment and literacy rates in the 1870s to 1890s

	Rate of	
	Enrollment	**Literacy**
Norway	.64	.98
Denmark	.70	.99
Finland	.10	.89
Sweden	.65	.98
Nordic average	.52	.96
Non-Nordic European average	.56	.82
New World average	.69	.80

Source: O'Rourke and Williamson (1995c: table 3)

Comparisons of enrollment and literacy rates from this period show that the Norwegian educational system was producing a level and scope of education in the 1870s to 1890s that was similar to that found in other Scandinavian countries, but significantly higher than in the rest of Europe. In particular, as evidenced in Table 3.1, it has been estimated that Norwegian enrollment and literacy rates were as high as 64 per cent and 98 per cent, while the non-Nordic European scores in these areas was just 56 per cent and 82 per cent, respectively.

In spite of this new activity on the part of the state, its direct involvement in the domestic economy remained relatively small by contemporary standards. Nevertheless, government expenditures were growing in proportion to the ambitions of public officials. In the first half of the 19th century the primary source of government revenue was the collection of import and export tariffs. After 1892, however, the state was able to draw on a newly introduced income tax. As a result, the state found it easier to secure revenues for expanding its services across the country: its expenditures (at both the national and local level) grew relatively quickly. While the total public expenditures of the Norwegian state in the 1870s totaled about seven per cent of what we would today refer to as Norway's national income (in other words, the total income generated by capital and labor for the whole country), it had risen to double that (about 14 per cent) by 1914 (Øien 1963: 182). Although this increase in public expenditures was undoubtedly a concern for many contemporaries, it is rather modest by today's standards.

Finally, the close of the 19th century saw the birth of a Norwegian labor movement with a reputation for radicalism. While this movement drew heavily from the experiences of similar movements in Scandinavia (and Europe more generally), its radicalism can be traced to some of the more unique features of the Norwegian economic landscape. In particular, the very tardiness of Norwegian industrialization meant that the indigenous labor movement was relatively late in developing. More significantly, perhaps, was the nature and location of Norwegian industrial development. In contrast to what is found in the rest of Scandinavia (and on the continent), the power base of the Norwegian labor movement was *not* located in urban areas, of which Norway had relatively few. Norway's labor movement took hold in the periphery, where its lumber, mining, hydroelectric and fishing industries were found. Finally, many of the new industries were capital — not labor — intensive, so they did not at first generate a large industrial working class.

The roots of a Norwegian labor movement can be traced to a small newspaper editor, Marcus Thrane (1817-1890). Riding the wave of revolutionary fervor that swept across Europe in the mid 1800s, Thrane led Norway's first organized popular movement, representing 414 associations, with over 30,000 members. While it began as a protest organization of workers, day laborers, and urban craftsmen, the movement quickly spread to include crofters, landless agricultural laborers and the petty peasantry, embracing many of the traits that we often associate with the English Charterists. Their demands were simple, if threatening to the establishment: the right to work, the right to property and the right to capital. Indeed, Thrane's success in organizing effective protests was rewarded in July 1851 when Thrane (along with about 200 of his followers) was placed under arrest and indicted for 'crimes against the security of the state'. After a lengthy imprisonment, from 1851 to 1858, Thrane fled to the United States in 1863, where he spent the last 27 years of his life.

While the authorities managed to place a cap on the Thrane movement, by imprisoning or banishing its most boisterous members, a new threat to the status quo began to develop at the end of the century in the new industries that dotted Norway's coastline. This nascent labor movement was eventually absorbed by the status quo, but the process was neither easy nor swift. Indeed, in the years immediately prior to (and following) World War I, the Norwegian labor movement spouted some of the most radical rhetoric on the continent (whether the movement was as radical as its rhetoric is another question altogether)!

Thus far, I have emphasized the relatively weak nature of the Norwegian establishment — a consequence largely of the Norwegian landscape (in particular, the difficulty in establishing large landed estates, where political and economic power could be concentrated). But a new establishment was taking hold in the

Norwegian capital, and its effectiveness and strength was clearly evident in its response to the threat posed by the Thrane movement.

The growing influence of rising economic elites can be seen in the effective organization and strategy of Norway's fledgling interest organizations: the *Landsorganisasjonen* (LO) and the *Norsk Arbeidsgiverforening* (NAF). The LO, founded in 1899, gathered various union groups together under a central organizational umbrella; the NAF was founded the following year (1900) as a counterpart to the LO, to represent the interests of business owners. Together these two organizations, in concert with the government, came to play a central role in subsequent political and economic developments.

While we tend to think of Scandinavian corporatist arrangements[5] in terms of the relative strength of its peak labor organization, the organized interest of Norwegian capital was relatively stronger than that of labor before World War I. This strength is evident in two related indicators of organizational capacity. The first concerns membership: the NAF represented firms that employed more workers than were represented by the LO! For example, in 1902 the NAF organized industrial concerns that employed 34,000 workers, while the LO could only entice 7,500 members that year. Although the LO was making substantial headway, it remained smaller than the NAF until after World War I.

The NAF was not averse to using its numerical superiority to secure favorable agreements. Indeed, Norwegian business owners pursued a more aggressive lock-out strategy than elsewhere in Scandinavia, and this—in turn—had significant consequences for the subsequent development of corporatist relations in Norway. This is the second indicator for the strength of Norwegian capital at the time. In particular, a rise in the number and spread of labor conflicts (see Figure 3.3) encouraged both partners to pursue an alternative means for resolving industrial disputes and emboldened the Norwegian government to play a more active role.

I do not mean to suggest that the Norwegian labor movement was static at the time. To the contrary, LO membership exploded during the first decade of the 20th century: from 1900 to 1907, its membership grew from about 5,000 to 40,000 (and it climbed to almost 68,000 by the eve of World War I). It is from this position of growing numerical strength that the Norwegian labor movement could force its (employer) counterpart to the negotiation table. But numerical strength was not enough: it needed to deliver what it promised. To do this, it needed a streamlined, hierarchical and centralized form of organization. These two qualities helped the LO to secure the first national wage agreement between the Norwegian Iron and Metal Workers and the NAF in 1907.

---

[5] Corporatism traditionally refers to a particular pattern of interest articulation, where organizations representing monopolistic functional interests (for example, the LO and NAF) engage in political exchange with state agencies over public policy. See, for example, Katzenstein (1985) and several contributions in Schmitter and Lehmbruch (1979). In Norway, corporatism did not really develop until the interwar period and only blossomed after the Second World War. But the seeds to this fruition were being planted before World War I.

While the 1907 agreement legitimized the LO's right to bargain on behalf of its workers, it did not resolve the differences that continued to separate workers and employers. Labor conflicts began to take on a more national characteristic, with drastic consequences for the entire economy. Indeed, the government's role in arbitrating Norwegian labor disputes was borne in response to the then largest conflict, when the NAF reacted to a local strike with a nationwide lock-out of all workers in the paper and cellulose industry (about 6,000 workers in all). Although the dispute was short-lived, and the workers proved eventually victorious, its potential for disruption drove the government to consider compulsory arbitration. In 1911, a Liberal government intervened to stop the largest conflict yet (this time involving more than 32,000 workers in the iron, mining, lumber and paper industries), and by 1912 compulsory arbitration had become a major point in the Liberal Party's election program (the largest and most influential party at the time). By 1916, the Liberals were able to force through a compulsory arbitration into law (to stave off a threatened national lock-out in 1916).

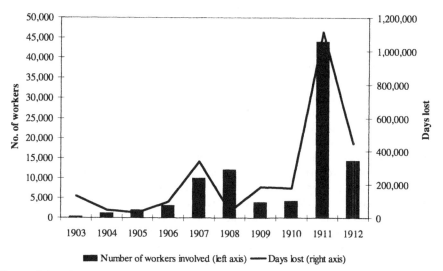

Figure 3.3   Prewar work stoppages

Source: Pax (2003)

In short, Norway developed a unique organizational setting for resolving labor disputes. Not only were the partner organizations strong, hierarchical and centralized, but they were willing to use their respective positions of power to secure general agreements. This centralized system encouraged the active involvement of the state in the form of compulsory arbitration (indeed, before the arrival of World War I, the parliamentary leader of the Labor Party would come to sit on the court of arbitration). When arbitrated solutions were seen as unfavorable to either party (as the 1911 solution appeared to workers), however, the legitimacy of the entire system was called into question.

Such was the situation after 1911, when an opposition movement began to openly question the centralization of the Norwegian LO, and its willingness to cooperate with the political authorities. This resistance is captured in the public's imagination by a colorful house-painter from Trondheim, Martin Tranmæl (1879 - 1967); its organizational form was the 'Trade Union Opposition Group of 1911'.

Tranmæl's radicalism was informed by an earlier visit to the United States, where he had been introduced to the syndicalism of the International Workers of the World (IWW). On returning to Norway, he advocated an alternative organizational form and strategy for the Norwegian labor movement. In particular, his movement called for the abandonment of collective agreements, the dissolution of labor insurance funds, and encouragement for the use of strikes, boycotts, cooperation and sabotage as weapons in the class struggle. Obviously, this did not make the Trondheim group particularly popular with the authorities.

The radicalism of the Trade Union Opposition Group did exert an influence upon the political organization of the nascent Norwegian labor movement. While the Norwegian Labor Party (DNA) had been constituted in 1887 — under the leadership of Christian Holtermann Knudsen (a typesetter from Bergen) and Carl Jeppsen (a cigar maker from Denmark) — it was rather weak and ineffective in its early years. At the time, the party could easily ride on the electoral coattails of the influential Liberal Party.

By 1894, the DNA was ready to compete in its first election, although it did not manage to secure parliamentary representation until 1903. Characteristic of Norwegian conditions, this representation (in the form of five socialist seats in parliament) was won from Northern Norway, in the wake of a riot against a whaling company. Quickly, however, the electoral attractiveness of the DNA took hold: in 1906 it won 16 per cent of the ballot, and this new influence was used to secure unanimous support in the Storting for the idea of compulsory arbitration of labor disputes. By 1915, the DNA's share had increased to 32 per cent, and it was poised to grab power in the interwar period (see Figure 3.2 above).

After the Russian Revolution, Tranmæl's movement effectively captured control of the DNA, and in 1918 the party congress voted to transform the party into a revolutionary party of class struggle. By the following year, the DNA was formally affiliated with the Comintern, and the LO joined the Amsterdam International. The Norwegian labor movement even tried to establish soviets between 1918 and 1920, although such efforts typically failed. It was not until the interwar period, in 1923, that the DNA chose to leave the Cominterm, and the party split into a minority Communist Party and a majority, more mainstream, DNA.

In short, the Norwegian labor movement was beginning to make its institutional presence felt in Norway by the end of the period under consideration. The DNA would come to play an absolutely central role in the post World War II rebuilding of Norway. Indeed, the Norwegian historian, Jens Arup Seip (1963), would come to refer to the postwar period in Norway (until 1965) as an era of the one-party state, where the one party was the DNA. But in the period under consideration, prior to World War I, the party remained relatively insignificant and on the margins of political power. As we shall discuss in the closing epilogue chapter, the party's fate would change drastically in the interwar period, when it was invited to form its first government.

Conclusion

My objective with this chapter has been to provide an institutional context for interpreting Norway's rapid economic catch-up prior to World War I. As such it is an ambitious chapter, one that attempts to cover a great deal of historical and conceptual territory. With all of its complexity, this institutional context can be understood as another very important backdrop (like the global backdrop described in Chapter 2), against which we can interpret the chapters that follow. In particular, I have aimed to paint—in broad strokes—the way in which Norway's institutional context is not unlike those that influence the choices available to many of today's developing states.

It may surprise most readers to learn that Norway's institutional, political and economic developments were clearly influenced by its subservient relationships to both Denmark and Sweden. Like many of today's developing states, and unlike most of Europe's development experience, Norway's early relationship to the world economy was channeled through ties of dependence that affected the nature, direction and pace of its economic development.

Another important commonality with today's developing states is the degree to which Norwegian economic development has relied heavily on the extraction of primary natural resources. It is in part because of this reliance that Norwegian industrialization was relatively tardy in the European context. As a consequence, early Norwegian production was also technically retarded—they were unable to adopt the latest and most productive technologies. When industrialization finally did arrive, it was directed at better exploiting Norway's comparative advantage in natural resources.

This is not to ignore the good fortunes that Norway did enjoy. Her relationship with Denmark helped to establish a strong rule of law [*rechtsstaat*], respect for property rights, a functioning judicial system and a stable economic infrastructure. The Norwegian landscape and climate may have cursed its farmers, but it also provided a number of remarkable opportunities: an abundance of fish, timber and hydroelectric power, for example. Indeed, the most important legacy of this rocky, mountainous landscape may have been how it spared Norway from the sort of feudal relationships that came to dominate in the rest of Europe.

Norwegian economic catch-up occurred in an ideological climate that was not unlike our own. Liberal political and economic thought was on the rise, and both the Norwegian economy and the world economy at large can be depicted in liberal terms. For a number of complicated reasons, including Norway's size and external dependency, Norway pursued a liberal economic strategy—encouraging the free trade of goods, services, investments and (increasingly) migration.

But this 19th century liberalism was quite different from our variant, as it appeared to allow for more domestic autonomy. While most Norwegian economic policies can be understood in terms of the doctrine of classic liberalism (for example, free trade in goods, services, and labor, and a small government budget), the nascent democratic state in Norway was still able to encourage and influence investments in local infrastructure, to finance significant industrial projects, and to protect and insulate infant industries from foreign competition and ownership. The details of this political involvement will be provided in the chapters that follow.

In short, what is perhaps most unique about Norway's institutional context is the way in which the country was willing to mix a largely liberal attitude to political and economic development with an increasingly active role for the state and important social institutions for regulating the nature and pace of that development. Indeed, a centralized state tradition was already beginning to take hold before the period under consideration; after 1814 this state is captured by civil servants ('the civil servants' state' [*embetsmannsstaten*]), who expanded the state's scope of activity.[6] Later on, Norwegian capital and labor interests (in league with the government) were able to agree on a process of mediation and cooperation that would later become a basic component of social democratic economic strategy. Finally, the early development of Norwegian concession laws allowed the state an active role in encouraging domestic production and ownership in the most important economic sectors. This allowed infant Norwegian producers a degree of protection that was used to secure the knowledge and experience that would eventually allow these producers the experience they would need to compete internationally.

---

[6] See, for example, Seip (1974 and 1981), Sejersted (1984 and 1993), and Slagstad (1998).

Chapter 4

Natural Bounty

Industrialization came late to Norway.

There are many reasonable explanations for this. First, and most glaringly, Norway lacked major coal deposits—the most significant fuel at the time—and its iron ore reserves were tucked away in difficult-to-reach places. Without access to these two great agents of early industrialization (coal and iron), Norway had difficulty catching the first wave of industrial developments. In addition, Norway lacked a strong and commercial agriculture sector—its climate and terrain made it difficult to generate the sort of rural surplus that could be stored, invested or exported to foreign markets. As we know from the broader European experience, it is from this agricultural surplus that a nascent bourgeoisie is born. The inadequacies of domestic agriculture led to other (related) handicaps, such as a poor infrastructure (for example, Norway lacked a stable domestic banking system and an efficient transportation network). To make matters worse, Danish and Swedish officials were openly skeptical about the Norwegians' ability and/or capacity to incorporate technical thinking. Even Norway's own Ministry of Finance doubted that its industries could compete with foreign factories (Finansdepartementet 1842: 45).

When industrialization did come to Norway, it did so after its traditional economic sectors (fish, lumber, agriculture and shipping) had already begun a remarkable transformation. Because of this, Norway's economic catch-up can be divided into two phases. The first, primary sector, phase lasted until the closing decade of the 19th century, and delivered respectable growth rates (of the order of—roughly—three per cent, per annum). The second phase began at the turn of the century, and was driven by significant investment in new technologies that exploited Norway's abundance of cheap hydroelectric power. While both phases drew from Norway's natural bounty, it is during this (second) phase that Norway's industrial transformation really took-off.

This chapter aims to describe both phases, covering the period 1865 to 1914. I begin with a brief discussion of the different approaches to explaining an economy's industrial transformation. I then turn to a broad empirical overview of the changes that shook the Norwegian economy, and briefly compare Norway's transition with other states that were undergoing similar adjustments. Finally, I describe some of the most important developments in the domestic economy prior to World War I: first in the traditional sectors, then in the new industrial sectors.

My objectives are twofold. First and foremost, I wish to elaborate on the role played by the three main motors of the Norwegian economy at the time: farming, fishing and shipping. Although changes in these three sectors are all linked to international markets (links that will be developed in the following chapter), their impact on Norwegian industrialization and subsequent economic development is of such importance that they deserve special attention.

In addition, I wish to illustrate the remarkable change-over that occurred in the Norwegian economy. At the beginning of the 19th century, Norway resembled an underdeveloped country of today: it suffered a low standard of living, a shortage of capital, and a system of production that was based mostly on self-sufficiency.   Norwegian production drew mainly from old and primitive techniques, producing low yields from undeveloped natural resources. This depiction of the Norwegian economy would hardly be recognizable in 1914.

Approaches to industrialization

The economic literature on industrialization, development and economic take-off is enormous, unwieldy, and largely irrelevant for understanding Norway's experience. Indeed, the Norwegian experience fits only uncomfortably with the many stylized models of economic transformation. Her transformation was based on the exploitation of natural resources in a political climate that was part liberal, part neo-mercantilist. Still, this uniqueness has not stopped economic historians from employing the Norwegian case as support (or as a spoiler) for various approaches to economic growth and industrial transformation. Neither should it stop us from providing a very rough road map of the different paths to industrialization.

Much of the academic literature on Norway's economic history is divided between those who focus on internal versus external determinants of economic growth. The former group tends to focus on demographic and legal developments over the course of the 19th century. The latter group emphasizes international trade and investment flows. Although I favor the external-determinants approach in a small country such as Norway, I do not wish to ignore important domestic factors, and this chapter aims to survey many of them. Indeed, both approaches are reasonable and offer significant insights into Norway's economic development. As with most academic disputes, the differences here are mostly over matters of emphasis, not content.

What each author and approach is trying to measure is an almost magical transformation of the economy where growth and productivity levels rise and the community begins to employ a new sort of economic logic. This is the same magic that marveled Adam Smith as he examined the ways in which productivity was improved by the division of labor, increasingly sophisticated worker skills, and the application of new production technologies:

> This great increase of the quantity of work which, in consequence of the division of labour, the same number of people are capable of performing, is owing to three

different circumstances: first to the increase of dexterity in every particular workman; secondly, to the saving of time which is commonly lost in passing from one species of work to another; and lastly, to the invention of a great number of machines which facilitate and abridge labour, and enable one man to do the work of many (Smith 1776: book I, chapter 1).

This transition reveals itself in terms of a remarkable transformation of the economy. While the details of each transition are always unique, there are several common features of countries undergoing them. One of these is the notion of transformation, or 'take-off', associated with W.W. Rostow (1960). Rostow's economic take-off is usually captured in a very specific way by pointing to a definite, discontinuous and sustained drive in real output per capita, made possible by a marked increase of the aggregate saving-income ratio. But we need not confine ourselves to such a narrow and technical definition of the term. Rather, we might borrow Rostow's concept to describe, simply, Norway's rapid industrial growth at the turn of the century.

Central to this transformation is a demographic movement from the countryside to the cities in search of industrial employment. In Arthur Lewis' (1954) influential argument, economic development is brought about by encouraging the large 'reserve army' of labor in the rural-based agricultural sector to move and provide cheap labor to the urban-based industrial sector. Indeed, many economists use rural employment as a rough indicator for industrialization: a country that employs less than 50 per cent of its workers in the primary sector (agriculture, forestry and fishing) is said to be industrialized. By this (admittedly rough) definition, Norway became industrialized in the 1890s (see Table 4.1 below).[1]

Economic highpoints

I think it is most helpful to begin with a general overview of developments in the Norwegian economy. Such an overview can capture the general pattern of economic activity during the period (for example, growth in GDP, inflation, and employment) and allow us to compare these developments with other countries making similar transformations.

Having said this, the fact that Norway was undergoing a structural adjustment (as it adopted a more productive industrial foundation) makes it relatively difficult to characterize the whole period in aggregate terms. Generally, economic activity in 1865-1914 can be characterized by significant economic growth, but this growth was also punctuated by price instability over extended periods.

---

[1] Of course, there is little consensus among economic historians on the exact date of Norway's industrial transformation. See Hovland and Nordvik (1997) for a review along these lines.

The first difficulty in capturing the nature of this economic activity is to choose an appropriate indicator. If we use GDP figures, the period can be depicted in terms of remarkable economic growth, with only a few single instances (individual years) of economic downturn. However, as Norway's population was growing steadily throughout this period (despite significant emigration), the country's growth rate is less impressive if we use GDP/capita figures. Indeed, choosing a per capita indicator will reveal that there were several years of negative growth in the period under consideration.

Because of these differences in indicators, it makes sense to consider demographic developments briefly. Over the previous four centuries, Norway's population had grown by only one half of one per cent a year; but this rate had doubled in the 1800s (although it dropped down again in the 1900s). Most of this trend can be explained by access to better food (for example, the power of the potato) and advances in public and private health/hygiene measures. Indeed, 19th century Norway had one of the highest rates of population growth in Europe. At the beginning of the 20th century, Norway was populated by roughly two and a quarter million people, and its population was still growing fast. This sort of impressive demographic growth means that changes in nominal and per-capita economic figures can be quite different.

With this caveat in mind, it is perhaps easiest to grasp the aggregate picture of economic activity by looking at the nominal GDP figures over time. Figure 4.1 draws on two trends to illustrate the way in which the overall picture is one of economic expansion as well as periods of fluctuating price levels. If we look at the GDP indicator (the solid line), we see only six brief periods when Norway experienced a real drop in economic activity—most of these declines lasted for just a single year.[2] Indeed, the longest period of decline covered only two years (1881-3), and this decline was relatively small, as illustrated in the figure. Quite remarkably, Norway's GDP more than doubled in the 1865-1914 period, growing from 28,431 million to 79,519 million kroner (in constant 2000 prices). The GDP indicator also reveals that the rate of increase grew significantly in the latter years (and, because of emigration, it was even stronger when measured in GDP/capita terms)! More impressive yet is the fact that Norway's levels of foreign trade and investment were increasing even more than its GDP during this period.

At the same time, the other (dotted line) indicator in Figure 4.1 shows that the period was also plagued by rapidly changing price levels. This is one of the most unique characteristics of the first 'Great Depression'. While GDP was mostly growing over the entire period, prices were falling for a significant amount of time around 1880. At the same time, this indicator (depicting the Consumer Price Index, or CPI, for the period, where 100=1920) shows how prices were also rising at the very beginning and end of the period, in tandem with Norway's economic expansion.

---

[2] In particular: 1867-8; 1869-70; 1887-78; 1881-82; 1882-3; and 1902-3.

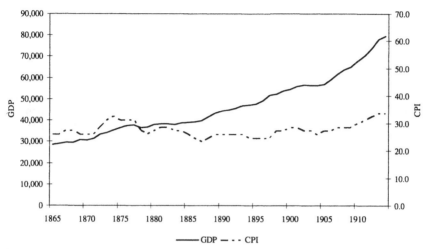

Figure 4.1   GDP and CPI, 1865-1914*

*Gross Domestic Product (GDP) is measured in millions of (constant 2000) kroner, using the left-hand axis. The Consumer Price Index (CPI) is set for 100 in the year 1920 and is read using the scale on the right-hand axis. As the axes scales are set arbitrarily, great caution should be used in interpreting the two indicators. This depiction is used to facilitate comparisons in trends, not levels.

Sources: GDP data is from SSB (2004); the CPI data is from Norges Bank (2004)

Comparatively speaking, Norway's growth was particularly strong. The work done by O'Rourke and Williamson (1995b) illustrates the strength of the Scandinavian economic record during this period.[3]   Although Norway was outperformed by Sweden and Denmark on several of these indicators, all three countries shared the same basic (liberal) attitude with respect to international trade and investments—and all three tended to do quite well. Norway's real GNP per capita was growing by 1.35 per cent over the period 1870-1913, while for the rest of (non-Scandinavian) Europe the average growth rate was only 0.91. Outside Scandinavia, only Germany (1.30) and Switzerland (1.32) came close to this sort of growth rate. Even more remarkably, Norway's real wage growth per urban worker in the period 1870 to 1913 was a whopping 2.46—this compares to the non-Scandinavian European average of 0.90, and a New World average of 0.92! Indeed, no country in Europe underwent real wage growth that was even close to that experienced by Norway, Sweden or Denmark.   Finally, this remarkable economic growth, especially in the years immediately prior to World War I, meant that factor prices converged dramatically between Scandinavia and the more

---

[3] The figures in this paragraph come from O'Rouke and Williamson (1995b: 290).

developed countries. In short, Norway (and Scandinavia) outperformed the rest of the OECD club (and probably the rest of the world) in the late 19th century.

This economic transformation pulled Norway from the poverty in which it was mired. But before we turn to describe these developments in more detail, it may be useful to remember how far Norway has come, and how similar these early Norwegian conditions were to those in the developing world today.

One of the most poignant indicators of poverty is an individual's expected lifespan. When Eilert Sundt wrote *Om Dødeligheden i Norge* [On Norway's Death-rate] in 1855, he noted that the average age of death was about 44 (for men, 47 for women). In 1910, conditions had improved such that Norwegian men were expected to live to be about 55 years of age, women to 58 (Hodne and Grytten 1992: 119). By contrast, Norwegians today tend to die at the age of 79. Still, many of today's poorest countries have a life expectancy at birth of around 35 years (the lowest is Mozambique, where the average life expectancy at birth is 31.3 years)![4]

Another common indicator of poverty is the number of people sharing a room. In many poor countries today, such as in Pakistan and India, three people—on average—share a room (in 1990's Norway, by contrast, the corresponding number was 0.6). But an 1858 investigation of working class housing conditions in Oslo found an average of four persons per room and three families to every kitchen.[5] Over the next quarter of a century, when Oslo doubled the number of its inhabitants, the new housing built was normally occupied at the rate of one family to each room (Derry 1973: 132).

Finally, it may surprise younger readers to discover that Norway was not impervious to child labor during its early years of industrialization. In 1875, an official inquiry recorded that 2,565 boys and 561 girls—all of them under fifteen and some under ten, provided eight per cent of the labor force for all of Norway's nascent factory industries. Some industries were more susceptible than others: for example, child labor represented 18 per cent of glass-workers; 33 per cent of match-making; and 43 per cent of tobacco workers' total labor force. Evidently, this was not seen to be such a very serious problem, as it took 17 years before this inquiry produced any legislative result (Derry 1973: 133).

Primary transformation

These aggregate figures tend to hide the enormous structural changes that were occurring in the Norwegian economy at the time. Traditional industries were modernizing and new industries were developing rapidly, especially after 1880.

---

[4] The contemporary comparative figures in this paragraph (and the next) come from *NationMaster* (2004).

[5] Eilert Sundt (1858) *Om Piperviken og Ruselökbakken*. This study was published as a supplement to *Folkevennen*; a full account of the book is given by Christophersen (1962: 182-205).

These changes are perhaps most evident in the radical drop-off in the percentage of Norwegians employed in the primary sector (for example, in farming, fishing and whaling), as evidenced in Table 4.1. While the percentage of employees in the primary sector dropped from 59.8 per cent in 1865 to 35.8 per cent in 1930, new jobs were being created in the secondary and tertiary sectors, by new — more productive — industries. By 1910, these traditional sectors contributed to less than a quarter of Norwegian GDP.

As we shall see below, many of these new industries exploited Norway's access to cheap and abundant electrical energy. But this new energy source also revolutionized production in many of the traditional sectors and created a number of new firms. Indeed, investments during the period 1900-1920 grew by 4.8 per cent annually (in contrast to a GDP growth rate of just 2.9 per cent) and new companies were popping up like weeds: of the 3,821 registered companies in 1909, 602 of them were established between 1900 and 1904, while another 698 were established in the following five years (Hodne and Grytten 1992: 44-5).

**Table 4.1   Labor force by industry (per cent of GDP in parentheses*),
percentage distribution for selected years, 1865-1930**

	1865	1875	1890	1900	1910	1930
Agriculture, forestry, fishing	59.8	51.8	49.2	40.7	39.0	35.8
and whaling	(45.3)	(35.4)	(31.6)	(25.0)	(23.7)	
Mining, manuf., construction,	13.6	18.1	21.9	26.3	25.0	26.5
electricity, gas & water	(17.8)	(21.8)	(24.3)	(28.0)	(26.2)	
Transport and communication	5.1	7.7	7.2	7.1	7.4	8.3
	(9.7)	(13.6)	(11.7)	(11.0)	(11.3)	
Trade, banking and insurance	2.8	3.5	5.0	6.5	7.1	10.5
	(8.6)	(10.1)	(13.3)	(16.3)	(17.8)	
Other private and public	12.6	14.2	15.3	16.7	17.8	18.6
services	(18.6)	(19.1)	(19.1)	(19.7)	(21.0)	
Industry unknown	6.1	4.7	1.4	2.7	3.7	0.3

*GDP figures before 1910 were calculated on the assumption of constant ratios between gross produce per employee in different industries.

Source: Labor force figures: SSB (1966: 54, table 21); GDP at current prices by industry: SSB (1966: 55, table 23).

Most impressively, the traditional sectors were transforming themselves and becoming more market-oriented and productive in response to changes that were largely sparked by developments in the international economy. These changes came to revolutionize the traditional sectors, freeing up excess labor that would eventually find its way into the new, even more productive, sectors of Norway's industrial economy.

Nowhere is this more evident than in Norway's agricultural transformation. Norwegian agriculture had remained relatively primitive for a number of reasons. The difficulty of communicating across Norway's rugged landscape meant that Norwegian peasants had little opportunity to learn of new agricultural ideas, and Norway never experienced an enclosure movement as was common elsewhere in Europe. Indeed, in many parts of the country people continued to employ collective farming measures, despite the dwindling size of farms (a result of inheritance into smaller and smaller units). In short—and despite drastic improvements over time—Norway's agricultural sector was contributing little to her economic development: it was hardly able to support its own growing population.

As was the case in most of Europe, Norway's agricultural transformation was sparked by the arrival of cheap grain from the New World. When Britain repealed its Corn Laws in 1846, it set in motion a ripple effect that was broadcast across the rest of Europe. To be sure, Norway's geography and climate assured it great benefit from the increased access to cheap grain. Norwegians realized this and reduced their grain tariffs in 1851 before dropping them all together in 1869. As a consequence, Norwegian corn imports increased five fold between 1850 and 1890; by the turn of the century, two thirds of its demand was being met by imports (Bergh et al. 1983: 47).

With access to cheap international grain, more and more Norwegian farmers moved into new areas, especially meat and dairy farming. Although the number of domesticated animals in Norway did not increase radically (as we might expect), their production levels per animal and slaughter weights did. Agricultural production increased rapidly, as farmers became better educated and implemented new and more productive techniques.[6]

This new emphasis on education is clearly evident in the establishment of the first advanced school of agriculture (in 1854) and the first scientific agricultural college in 1897, both in the village of Ås. The transformation also coincided with the rise to a new cooperative movement which began to exert real influence in the closing decades of the century (and even more so in the interwar period, as we shall discover in Chapter 9). The new concentration on dairy farming led to the development of cooperative-dairies that came to dominate the industry: in 1900, 669 of the 775 dairies (or 86 per cent) were cooperative (Bergh et al. 1983: 57). Other organizational movements, such as the Farmers' Federation [*Landmandforbundet]* and the Smallholders' Association [*Småbrukarlaget*] grew quickly and became formidable pressure groups on social and cultural issues.

By the turn of the century, a better-educated, better-organized, and better-equipped modern agriculture sector was poised to exploit the fruits of its

---

[6] Hodne and Grytten (2000: 183) hold that agricultural productivity was 2.5 times higher in 1910 than it was in 1835. The largest growth occurred between 1865 and 1875, and the first decade of the 20th century.

productive transformation. From 1900 to 1920, the Norwegian agriculture community enjoyed an 'unusually long and prosperous period of progress' (Fuglum 1978: 233).

This increase in agricultural productivity had important spillover effects on Norway's broader industrialization project. When productivity increased on the farms, peasants could move to the city to take on better-paying and more productive jobs. As late as 1845, 84.5 per cent of Norway's population still lived in agricultural districts. By 1900 the number had dropped to 64 per cent and by 1920 only 54.4 per cent of the population continued to live in the countryside (Hodne 1981: 429).

Similar developments were evident in the timber industry, which functioned as a sister industry to Norwegian farming. (The Norwegian small farmer often supplemented his meager income with either fishing or forestry earnings.) In the timber industry, the main deterrent of change had been an old privilege system that protected the interests of those who controlled the waterfalls (which, in turn, drove the saw mills). When this system of privilege was dismantled in 1860, the industry underwent very rapid technological modernization. Later, a rise in the international demand for books, magazines and newspapers provided the Norwegian wood processing industry with an enormous boost. This new demand led to an intensive search for alternative ways to produce paper (especially newspaper) and in the 1870s, textile-fibers were replaced by wood pulp.

While the first production of mechanical pulp took place in Germany, Norway was quick to adopt the technology: exploiting its experience with saw mill technologies, its access to abundant timber reserves, and a new generation of mechanical engineers. Norwegian pulp was first exported in 1868 and reached its peak in the early 1870s, when annual exports reached two and one third million cubic meters. Norway's first cellulose factory was built in 1874, and by 1881 the country had 37 pulp mills and eight paper mills. In terms of employment, sawing and planning mills were the largest employers throughout the period (Derry 1973: 124), and in 1890, cellulose and wood pulp dominated Norwegian exports (in terms of value). While the value of this export in that year was set at 10,466,100 kroner, the next closest industrial export (nails and horseshoe nails) was worth only 3,333,250 kroner (Hodne and Grytten 2000: 207, table 13.2).

Indeed, the early years of Norwegian industrialization were dominated by the timber industry, and Norway's first large international concerns were in the wood processing industry. Paper and pulp were attractive investments for foreigners because of Norway's relatively small trees, its easy access to water turbines (and, later, cheap hydroelectric power), and its developed network of sawmills. For these reasons, Norwegians soon became industrial leaders in modern milling and wood-processing industries and they began to export people and technology to Russia and across Scandinavia.

Fishing was another dynamic component of the early Norwegian export economy, with very important spillover effects. Like work in the forests, coastal farmers often took to the sea to supplement meager agricultural incomes. In the last quarter of the 19th century there were two main fisheries drawing Norwegians to the sea: the cod fishery in the north and the herring fishery in the south.

The capital and technology needs of traditional Norwegian fishing were hardly overwhelming. Indeed, one of the most distinguishing characteristics of the Norwegian fishery at this time was its parochial nature. In contrast to developments on the continent, the capital needs of Norwegian fishermen were usually *not* met by an independent class of financiers. Instead, these needs were addressed by the local community or family. It was often the case that all participating fishermen contributed in common to the boat and equipment—and they then shared the catch in proportion to their contribution. This meant that Norwegian fishing tended to occur out of rather small, locally-owned, boats.[7]

While much of the fish was consumed, the largest share was caught for export. In fact, between 70 to 90 per cent of Norway's 19th century catch was exported in the form of dried fish, *klippfisk*,[8] salted fish, fish oil (cod liver oil), roe, and salted sardines by the barrel. Fish was one of Norway's most important export articles: in 1870, fish alone represented about half of Norway's total export value (albeit only four per cent of the country's GDP)—although this figure halved by the end of the century (Nerbøvik 1999: 71). While fish's share of exports reached its peak in the 1880s, export volumes continued to grow. After 1880, fishing's share of exports fell to 35 per cent; in the 1890s it fell below 30 per cent (Bergh et al. 1983: 75).

As in other sectors of the economy, Norwegian fishing underwent a technological revolution at the turn of the century. The advent of a more efficient, dependable and affordable combustion engine had a huge (if somewhat belated) effect on Norwegian fishing culture. With motors, coastal fishermen could extend their reach significantly, exploiting new fishing areas and reaping considerable safety gains. Here too, however, Norwegians were tardy at adopting the new technology. While the Danish fishing fleet in Skagen and Fredrikshaven was almost completely under motor power in 1900, there was only one motorized fishing smack in all of Norway. By 1914, however, Norway had made the transition to a motorized fleet: its fishing fleet consisted of 7,352 motor-driven, 1,972 sail-driven and 210 steam-driven boats (Hodne 1981: 127). Other new fishing technologies were adapted, giving rise to a phenomenal increase in the catch: from 308,000 tons in 1905 to 577,000 tons in 1914 (Nerbøvik 1999: 242). The cost of these technical improvements made it increasingly difficult for local

---

[7] This pattern begins to change in the early 20th century, as technical developments demanded larger and larger investments. To protect the small traditional coastal fisherman, a law was passed in 1908 that outlawed trawlers (except for prawns) in Norwegian waters. Like the small Norwegian farmer, the coastal fisherman has won a central place in the collective heart of modern Norway. Even as recently as the 1980s, two thirds of Norway's domestic consumption of fish was caught with small coastal fishing boats.

[8] *Klippfisk* is split and salted cod that was traditionally spread on rocks or special platforms for sun-drying.

communities to fund the industry: as a consequence, we see the establishment of a state bank for fishermen [*Statens Fiskarbank*] in 1921.

But the most significant technological development affecting the Norwegian fleet happened on land. The canning industry, especially the canning of brisling-sardines, came to replace the traditional way that Norwegian fish had been processed for export. While canning began as a labor-intensive industry, it was soon mechanized when a Stavanger mechanic, Heinrich Reinerts, launched a new patented factory in 1903. Between 1903 and 1915, the number of canning factories tripled; employment (in man hours) quadrupled; and exports grew *fourteen*-fold (Hovland 1995: 280)!

The Norwegian whaling industry grew out of the coastal fishing industry. Here the driving influence to hunt offshore was not the combustion motor, but a couple of significant inventions that help to explain Norway's leading role in this infamous profession. Two well-known entrepreneurs of the time illustrate the influence and focus of Norwegian whaling. Svend Foyn is known for several inventions to the detriment of marine mammals (including a purpose-built vessel for seal hunting—which he used to great economic advantage off the edge of the polar ice west of Jan Mayen Island—and a specially-designed steamboat for approaching whales). Most famous, however, was his (1868) invention of a harpoon gun for firing a missile which exploded inside the whale. For better or for worse, this deadly device was the first known Norwegian invention of world importance. Later in the first decade of the 20th century a second Norwegian inventor helped to change the face of modern whaling. Christen Christensen developed a factory ship, a 2,400-ton cargo boat, which he converted into a 'floating pier', making it possible to conduct whaling operations at the antipodes.

At the turn of the last century, whaling was a truly international industry. Whaling ships plied the seven seas, often in very inhospitable waters, in search of allusive and dangerous treasure. Norway's influential role in this sector reflects not only the ingenuity of her hunters (as illustrated by men such as Foyn and Christensen), but also a comparative advantage in one of her most important industries: shipping.

There is hardly a profession that is more central than sailing to the Norwegian ethos. Thus, Bjørnstjerne Bjørnson (the 1903 Nobel laureate in Literature) composed his 1868 'Song of the Norwegian Seaman', where:

> *Our glory and our might*
> *Are borne on sail-wings white.*

But the influence of shipping extends beyond Norway's poets. The role of the Norwegian shipping industry at this time is perhaps best illustrated by the fact that three leaders of the Norwegian Ship-owners' Association [*Norges Rederforbund*], founded in 1909, became influential prime ministers in Norway: Christian Michelsen, Gunnar Knudsen and Johan Ludwig Mowinckel. It is also clearly evident in the size of the export earnings generated by this influential sector (as we shall explore in more detail in Chapter 5).

As in the fishing sector, the shipping industry was built on a remarkably local ownership structure. The so-called *'Partsrederiet'* [cooperative ship-owners] or *'Folkerederiet'* [people's ship-owners] developed out of old cooperative ventures between the local sailing, shipbuilding, trade and handicrafts industries. A ship was, in effect, a sort of primitive corporation, with the community providing necessary capital and credit to keep it afloat.

At first glance, Norway's mastery of the sea appears remarkable for a country with so small a population. Between 1850 and 1880, the Norwegian fleet rose from being the eighth largest to the third largest fleet in the world, displacing 1,519,000 tons in 1880 (see Figure 4.2). Over the same period of time, Norway's sailing fleet expanded from 284,000 tons to 1,461,000 net tons; its number of sailors swelled to 62,000 by 1878. Despite its small size, however, Norway enjoyed an abundance in the most important inputs to the sailing industry: lumber (for boats), labor (for crews) and navigational competence (for survival). But Norway's comparative advantage in shipping could only be truly exploited once international trade and shipping markets were liberalized.

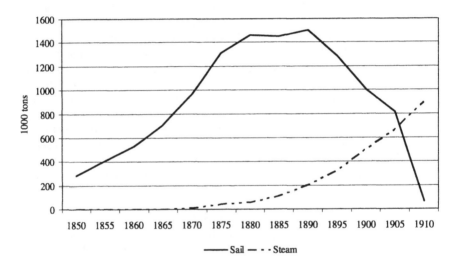

Figure 4.2   Norwegian shipping fleet, thousand tons

Source: Hodne (1973: 103)

Thus, the rise of Norwegian shipping followed a familiar pattern: it depended critically on the liberalization of foreign demand. Norwegian competence in shipping had developed over centuries of reliance on sea transport along Norway's long and rugged coastline. It had been fine-tuned with the export of Norwegian timber products during the 18th and 19th centuries. In fact, one of the great benefits to the free trade arrangement with Sweden was that Norway was allowed to circumvent the British Navigation Laws, and ship Swedish lumber between Britain and Sweden. When the British Navigation Laws were repealed on New Year's Day in 1850, Norway was posed to expand this activity to other trading states. Indeed, just five days later, the first of many Norwegian ships loaded with timber from Quebec arrived in London. The British example was followed by the Dutch, and other countries (such as France, Spain and Portugal) began to abolish differential charges against foreign carriers. As these countries began to employ foreign carriers, Norway was there to deliver the goods.

The Norwegian fleet's rapid and impressive growth is a function of how it had grown from simply carrying goods to and from Norwegian and Swedish harbors. By 1872, 80 per cent of Norwegian freight earnings stemmed from the international carrying trade. While the size of the fleet that served the carrying demands of the Norwegian economy had doubled during the years 1860-1880, the share that sailed exclusively in international trade had quadrupled (Hodne 1973: 99).

But Norway's position was precarious, as changes in technology would soon threaten her position. In 1870, five sixths of Norwegian freight was made up of timber (including much Swedish timber); the remainder was mostly tramp cargoes. Almost all of it (99 per cent) was delivered by sail. Indeed, in 1878 (nine years after the opening of the Suez Canal) the sailing tonnage under Norwegian ownership was still growing—in stark contrast to the fleets in other countries. In other words, Norway's reliance on cheap labor, old technology, and abundant timber made it dangerously conservative.

This conservatism proved to be expensive, and Norway paid through the nose with a long (30 years) crisis in Norwegian shipping. From 1878 to 1888, employment on Norwegian ships fell by almost 20 thousand men (Bergh et al. 1983: 106). Yet the size of the sailing fleet continued to rise before peaking in 1890 (at 1,503,000 net tons). Still, it was not until 1907 before steam tonnage outstripped sail (that is, 814,000 against 751,000 tons), as evidenced in Figure 4.2.

The resistance to change is easy to understand, if costly. Norway's long sailing tradition, its local ownership structure [*partsrederiet*] and its local wharf traditions all hampered an easy transition to steel and steam. This coalition of the conservative wrought an enormous economic crisis that began in Arendal in 1886 and spread across most of the Norwegian coastline from 1890 to 1910. It was in this climate of crisis that Norwegian shipping came about—but the locus of these changes was not in the traditional sailing ports of Southern Norway. Rather, it was an outward-looking Bergen that was able to attract sufficient amounts of capital and entrepreneurship to forge ahead as Norway's pace-setter in steam shipping. After all, Bergen had a long tradition for exporting fish (a market where haste and quality are prized attributes).

With the gradual introduction of stream, the Norwegian mercantile fleet was unable to absorb rural labor at the same rate as before 1876. For four straight decades the Norwegian labor force at sea had grown by more than 30 per cent per decade: from 11,279 men in 1835 to 60,281 men in 1875. In the following three decades, however, the number of Norwegian sailors began to decline: falling 0.1 per cent in 1875-1884, and falling six per cent and 8.9 per cent in the following two decades, respectively. In 1904 the number of men on board had dropped to about 50,000 sailors (Hodne 1973: 104).

This was not necessarily such a terrible thing, as life at sea was no piece of cake. Indeed, Norway's affinity at the time for old (and deteriorating) sailing ships did not improve matters. Nerbøvik (1999: 78) tells us that 2,515 sailors had defected from Norwegian ships in foreign harbors in the year 1888. Worse, the accident statistics in this profession were terribly high. Between 1884 and 1894, 2,182 Norwegian ships went under! In the worst year, 1894, a full tenth of the Norwegian fleet sunk, taking with it 567 sailors.

But when the alternative is unemployment, any lost job is a source of grief. Obviously, the crisis hit the older shipping centers in Southern Norway particularly hard; and it is here that we find some of the highest emigration rates to the New World in the 1880s and 1890s. Major sailing centers (in, for example, Rogaland, Vest-Agder and Øst-Agder) suffered the greatest outflow of rural emigrants. Indeed, emigration rates from southern Norway, where most of the sailing industry was based, were double the national average in the decade 1895-1904 (Hodne 1973: 105).

Industrial take-off

Norway's industrial transformation is unique in that it relied heavily on the development of cheap hydroelectric power. This development attracted foreign capital and skills, and encouraged new types of economic activity (that, in turn, relied heavily on cheap electrical inputs). It is these sorts of economic activities that propel Norway's impressive GDP growth after the turn of the century (as witnessed in Figure 4.1). As we have already noted in Chapter 3, the ownership structure of this new energy source was also quite unique: the Norwegian government was able to restrict foreign exploitation of its natural resources. Thus, by way of its concession laws, foreign capital and industrial development in Norway occurred under the watchful eyes of government officials. Apparently, the allure of Norwegian hydroelectric power was so strong that this government intervention did not deter foreign investors.

This is not to say that Norway lacked an industrial transformation in other sectors of the economy. As I have endeavored to show above, the traditional export sectors underwent significant changes during the early period of this study: farming, fishing, timber and shipping trades introduced new technologies that radically improved their productiveness and competitiveness. Still, I think it has been useful to divide Norway's economic transformation into two periods. Until 1890-1900, Norway's economic growth drew largely from modernizing her traditional (and core) economic activities. In the face of cheap grain imports, Norwegian farmers began to focus on animal husbandry. From the seeds of her traditional timber trade grew a modern wood pulp and cellulose industry. Atop her traditional reliance on the export of dried and smoked fish, Norway developed a modern canned fish industry. From the ashes of a slow and outdated wooden sailing fleet rose a modern, steel-hulled and steam-powered, shipping industry.

Given this two-phased transformation (one in the traditional sectors, the other heavily reliant on cheap hydroelectric power) it is rather pointless to look for any single causal factor that can explain Norway's economic take-off. In the 1860s, the Norwegian economy was still characterized by a remarkable degree of economic self-sufficiency: its rural sectors remained steeped in tradition and mostly removed from the rigors of any modern capitalist logic. As agricultural output was generally for local consumption, there was little need to think in terms of larger returns on investments, of accumulation, or of new techniques and increased productivity.

Whereas railway construction was helping to connect national markets in most other countries (and introduce important industrial technologies with their own spillover effects), the Norwegian railway-building program was necessarily modest. Norway's rugged landscape made it difficult and costly for the railway to reach outlying communities. Perhaps the closest substitute in Norway was the role played by the influential ship-building industry. Like railways, the ship-building industry was able to encourage a new engineering industry and a plethora of new machine shops. These new skills and technologies would come to play an important role in Norway's subsequent industrialization.

Most significant in encouraging Norwegian industrialization, perhaps, was the role played by the liberalization of British trade. If Great Britain had not liberalized its tariff policies and set aside her prohibitions on the export of machinery in 1842, or if she had not repealed her Corn Laws in 1846, or her Navigation Acts in 1849/50, it is difficult to imagine a Norwegian economic take-off. So much of Norway's economic transformation, especially in its first phase, was driven by changing demand in international markets. Most of these changes were, in turn, affected by British commercial policy.

This British influence is particularly obvious in Norway's first real industrial endeavor: the growth of a domestic textile industry. Once Britain's prohibition on the export of machines was lifted, Norwegian entrepreneurs began to flood into Britain to study the world's most modern and efficient cotton factories. These entrepreneurs eventually returned to Norway with knowledge of these new techniques, so that—by mid century—it was possible to detect a small Norwegian textile industry that was exploiting mass production techniques of standard goods for anonymous consumers. Already in the late 1840s there were six cotton-spinning mills in Norway, protected by legislation and reliant on imported inputs (machinery, cotton yarns) and borrowed technology.

But Norway's industrial footprint remained relatively small until the end of the century. In 1860 there were less than 20,000 men employed in industry, most were employed in the timber industry (31.8 per cent), others worked in the textile (15.4 per cent) and food and beverage (15.3 per cent) industries (Jörberg 1970: 72, table 23). Most of these industrial workers were employed in very small factory settings: 60 per cent of Norway's factories in 1895 employed fewer than 20 people (Lieberman 1970: 128).

In the 1870s this began to change. Between 1870 and 1875, the number of industrial workers increased by 14,000, or by nearly 50 per cent (Jörberg 1973: 429)! While this growth is impressive, it is largely based on humble beginnings.

After all, as we saw in Table 4.1, the mining, manufacturing, construction, gas and water sector employed only 18 per cent of the Norwegian labor force in 1875. Neither was this growth long-lasting: the 30 years that followed proved to be difficult. Economic growth per person came to a near standstill, as Norway was still experiencing significant demographic growth.

Thus, in the beginning, Norway's industrial transformation began by mimicking goods that were earlier imported (for example, textiles, nails, gate works, iron fencing, pots and pans). To use today's terms, her basic model was one of import substitution, not production for export. While there was strong and growing domestic demand for these goods, there was little hope that these domestic industries could compete with foreign competitors.

This attitude changed radically with the advent of cheap and plentiful electricity. As Lenin was famously aware, electrification was the key to a modern economy, and Norway was particularly well blessed with the natural resources that would provide cheap power. Because of this, Norway was able to attract foreign investors that could help her develop a modern hydroelectric industry. The resulting activity brought a remarkable transformation to the Norwegian countryside.

Although Norway was rich in waterfalls that could generate hydroelectricity, she lacked the high pressure turbine technologies that would allow her to capture and tame the power inherent to water falling several hundred meters. In the early years (as in nearly every other sector) this technology needed to be imported from abroad, as did the capital needed to fund the construction of installations that could generate, transform and transmit electric power at enormous scale. Enough of these conditions were met by 1896-1900, so that eleven sizeable hydroelectric plants were constructed, together with three steam generators and two in connection with gasworks. By 1908, the total installed electric power capacity in Norway was 200,000 kilowatts (kW); just four years later, in 1912, this figure surpassed 400,000 kW; and by 1920 it had already reached 1.25 million kW (Lieberman 1970: 138)

Some of these new power stations were enormous by the standards of the time. For example, when construction began in 1905 on the hydroelectric installation at Svelgfoss, it was to produce 30,000 horsepower—as much water-generated power as had been produced in Norway in the three previous years! At the time of its construction, the installation was Europe's largest (and the world's second largest).

This sort of cheap and abundant power propelled Norway's industrial take-off. As a result, she developed a modern, process-based factory industry that relied on large amounts of electric power and new electro-chemical and electro-metallurgical technologies.

The calcium carbide industry was one of the first to benefit from Norway's cheap energy. Calcium carbide was used mostly for the production of acetylene gas and could be produced by fusing lime together with a carbonaceous material in an electric furnace (the molten product needed to attain a temperature of about 2,000 degrees centigrade). When cooled, the carbide was crushed and packed in steel drums for export. As Norway enjoyed abundant reserves of both cheap power and high-grade limestone, it could quickly exploit the world's demand for calcium carbide. In 1910, Norway was already producing 50,000 tons (up from 2,000 tons in 1900) and supplying about 20 per cent of the world's demand (Lieberman 1970: 138-9). By 1913, 180,000 tons were being exported, to the tune of 33 million kroner—as much as the export value of Norwegian timber products (Holt et al. 1963: 383).

On the heels of a growing carbide industry, Norwegian firms began to produce a variety of ferroalloys (for example, silicomaganese, ferrosilicon, ferromanganese, and ferrochrome), drawing on domestic reserves of quartz and scrap iron. Like the carbide industry, the vast majority of Norwegian ferroalloys were being exported, mostly to the UK, Belgium and Germany. A third industrial product, aluminum, is obtained through a process of electrolysis in which a solution of aluminum oxide is subjected to heating at temperatures close to 1,000 degrees centigrade in a bath of cryolite. This process consumes a phenomenal amount of electrical energy. It was this demand for electricity that made aluminum production in Norway price-competitive, as (unlike the previous two examples) Norway had to import the other production inputs (bauxite or alumina).

Finally, and most influentially, Norwegian industry developed a cheap synthetic alternative to the world's dwindling supply of Chilean saltpeter (fertilizer). The Norwegian contribution rested on an electro-chemical process invented by Professor Kristian Birkeland at the University of Oslo, who succeeded in producing nitric acid by means of an electric arc.[9] In short, Birkeland showed how saltpeter could be made from nitrogen in the air, given massive amounts of electrical energy. The market value of Birkeland's discovery was soon recognized by one of Norway's foremost entrepreneurs at the time, Sam Eyde.

On the basis of Birkeland's invention, Eyde gathered an influential group of Norwegian entrepreneurs and Swedish financiers to create a holding company that could act as a decision-making center for the commercial exploitation of Bierkeland's invention. The resulting company, A/S Det Norske Aktieselskab for Elektrokemisk Industri—or *Elkem*, was born in 1904 and quickly became a giant of Norwegian industrial history. In the following year, Elkem spun off a daughter company, Norsk Hydro-Elektrisk Kvælstofakticselskab (*Norsk Hydro*), which was to exploit the Svelgfoss installation and had an option to acquire some of *Elkem*'s properties and patents. By 1906, *Norsk Hydro* had acquired the Notodden experimental nitrate plant from *Elkem*, and became permanently associated with Norwegian saltpeter.

As Eyde was the only Norwegian on *Norsk Hydro*'s board of directors, rumors soon began to circulate that foreign companies were starting a massive campaign to buy up Norwegian waterfalls. Indeed, as we shall explore in more detail in Chapter 6, most of the capital for these new heavy industries came from abroad, as Norway suffered from relatively small levels of domestic savings. The

---

[9] To be fair, it is probable that Professor Birkeland would rather be remembered as the man who unlocked the secrets of the aurora borealis. For a fascinating account of his life, see Jago (2001).

eventual consequence of these rumors was the approval of a parliamentary bill in 1906 that effectively prohibited the construction of hydroelectric plants without official permission (and regulating their sale to Norwegians). This was the start of the Norwegian concession laws already discussed in Chapter 3. Eyde's influence on the eventual legislation is fascinating, but (unfortunately) beyond the scope of this project.[10]

All of this new activity in the electric, chemical and metallurgical sectors brought a significant amount of economic stimulus to Norway's outlying districts (where the cheap energy was to be found). In 1909, there were 17 electrochemical and electrometallurgical factories, employing more than 2,000 workers. In addition, these industries provided a strong foundation for further scientific research in Norway. At first Norwegian technicians and engineers had to travel abroad for their education; by 1910 the demand for technical education became so strong (and important for Norway) that Norges Tekniske Høyskole was established in Trondheim (the predecessor to my own university, NTNU). Finally, and perhaps most importantly, these activities played a central role in Norway's new export-led growth strategy. This is the subject of the next chapter.

---

[10] For a longer discussion on Eyde's role in (and influence on) the concession laws, see Lieberman (1970: 136ff). For a more critical account of Eyde's influence, see Jago (2001).

Chapter 5

Trading Up

It is hard to exaggerate the importance of trade for a country like Norway. International trade is both essential and difficult for small under-developed countries. It is essential as the size of the domestic market is too small to be self-sufficient in many critical goods and services, and/or to exploit economies of scale. It is difficult because these countries often cannot generate the foreign reserves that they need to purchase necessary goods and services in international markets. Worse, these countries often find themselves at the mercy of international trends that influence their access to world markets. These are the sorts of issues this chapter will address, as they frame Norway's response to international trade before World War I.

In the last chapter I noted how Norway had difficulty producing enough food for its (now burgeoning) population. This problem of national self-sufficiency for small countries is most obvious when it comes to the production of food—but it is a problem that pervades many economic sectors. A small underdeveloped economy is generally unable to satisfy domestic demand and it must rely on the import of critical goods and services. As we shall see, during this period Norway relied heavily on the import of essential foodstuffs and production inputs.

While small-country reliance upon imported foodstuffs is fairly obvious, it is not always clear how these countries can pay for their critical imports. After all, a country has to have access to foreign reserves to purchase foreign imports (as we pay for foreign purchases with foreign currencies), and these can only be obtained by selling goods/services on the international market. In short, to be able to afford imports, a country has to be able to export something of value. For many countries, necessary imports (either for consumption or production inputs) are simply not affordable because of a shortage of foreign reserves: you have to pay to play. Norway's lucky solution to this dilemma was found in the foreign earnings of its shipping industry. Without these foreign earnings, Norway could not have afforded to import the materials that were necessary for her industrial transformation (and subsequent export).

But a small country must rely on exports for reasons other than obtaining foreign currencies. Most significantly, small countries cannot possibly generate enough domestic demand for domestic firms to exploit economies of scale. In order to compete with firms that enjoy larger domestic markets, small country producers need access to foreign demand. Only then can they realize the most effective production techniques, allowing them to specialize in areas where they enjoy a comparative advantage internationally.

For example, consider Norway's production of aluminum. Because of Norway's abundance of cheap hydroelectric power and easy access to the sea, Norway became a major producer and exporter of aluminum. Modern industrial products such as aluminum were central to Norway's industrial transformation— generating jobs, skills, and much-needed foreign currency. But this industry required a phenomenal amount of investment in necessary infrastructure (for example, to deliver massive amounts of electricity). Indeed, given Norway's relatively small domestic demand for aluminum, it is doubtful that any investor would have found it worthwhile to develop the industry without the possibility of export. Norwegian aluminum production was only cost-effective if it was free to satisfy international demand.

Aluminum production may be special in that it requires enormous amounts of investment capital. But almost all industrial production benefits from these kinds of economies of scale. After all, the larger the demand for a given product, the larger its potential revenue stream, and the better are the opportunities for exploiting international divisions of labor (as well as funding large research and development programs). This is the logic of large markets—a logic that requires small economies to join and participate in international markets and trade.

A vibrant export sector creates jobs that, in turn, spark domestic demand. Obviously, workers are paid to produce things made for consumption abroad. This domestic wage can then be used to stimulate the consumption of domestic goods (for example, housing, food and clothing), which—in turn—has multiplier effects throughout the rest of the economy. In other words, when an export worker spends his paycheck (and at this time, workers were mostly men), he provides a stimulus to local producers who sell him the food, clothes and housing he requires. This new demand stimulus, if large enough, can encourage local producers to expand their production, hiring more workers, who—in turn—purchase local goods and spread the wealth. This, in a nutshell, is the logic of an export-driven growth model. Countries can use a thriving export sector to generate economic growth and industrial transformation.

To exploit this model, a country needs access to three things: an international trading environment that minimizes tariffs and non-tariff barriers to trade; the capacity to produce something that the international community of trading states wants (at a price that it is willing to pay); and a coherent commercial strategy. After 1865, Norway enjoyed all three conditions. The first prerequisite was largely provided by Great Britain, as described in Chapter 2. This chapter will examine the latter two prerequisites to show how Norwegian commercial policy and production allowed it to exploit international markets to 'trade up' in the international community.

Trade theory

Before launching an empirical depiction of Norwegian trading patterns, it should prove useful to introduce some simple trade theory. This introduction aims to address two issues that underlie the empirical description that follows. The first has to do with the role of trade in a country's development strategy. The second has to do with deciding which goods a country should decide to trade (export and import). Both issues can be traced back to David Ricardo, and both were important considerations in the making of Norwegian commercial policy during this time.

Most modern trade theory builds on David Ricardo's (1817) *The Principles of Political Economy and Taxation*. Ricardo's claim to fame was in showing that all countries, not just the strongest producing countries, could benefit (relatively) from trade. This means that each country is better-off by trading, relative to not trading. By engaging in international trade, countries can enjoy the fruits of an increased division of labor and specialization:

> Under a system of perfectly free commerce, each country naturally devotes its capital and labor to such employments as are most beneficial to each. This pursuit of individual advantage is admirably connected with the universal good of the whole. By stimulating industry, by rewarding ingenuity, and by using most efficaciously the peculiar powers bestowed by nature, it distributes labor most effectively and most economically: while, by increasing the general mass of production, it diffuses general benefit, and binds together by one common tie of interest and intercourse, the universal society of nations throughout the civilized world. It is the principle which determines that wine shall be made in France and Portugal, that corn shall be grown in America and Poland, and that hardware and other goods shall be manufactured in England (Ricardo [1817] 1965: 77).

This belief in the relative gains from trade — what the Nobel prize-winning economist, Paul Samuelson, called 'the most beautiful idea in economics' — has become a central tenet of modern economics. It is one of the very few things upon which most economists can agree. For the reasons expounded upon in the introduction to this chapter, the utility of foreign trade for a small poor country (such as Norway before World War I) would appear to be abundantly clear.

But neo-Ricardian theory also provides clear lessons about what sort of goods and services a country can expect to import and export. On the backs of seminal contributions by Eli Heckscher, Bertil Ohlin and Paul Samuelson — and under a series of fairly restrictive assumptions — the Heckscher-Ohlin-Samuelson (H-O-S) model holds that a nation's comparative advantage is determined by the relative abundance and most profitable combination of its factors of production. In short, a country will export those commodities which are intensive in the use of its abundant factor (and import those commodities which are intensive in the use of its scarce factor).

The problem, of course, is in determining the factors of abundance in a given country. It is a no-brainer to argue (as Ricardo did in the quote above) that France and Portugal should export wine, while America and Poland should export grain. But what could a country like Norway export? In the broadest (and original) terms, the factors of production were labor, capital and land. At this level of aggregation, it is not easy to see how Norway could benefit from free trade. After all, Norway was a country poor in land (only three per cent of its land is arable), capital (as we shall see in Chapter 6, Norway came to rely heavily on foreign capital), and people (at the turn of the century Norway only had about two million people — a relative pittance by international standards). But Ricardian trade theory holds that even a poor country like Norway should benefit from increased trade.

The trick to neo-Ricardian trade theory is in operationalizing 'relative' abundance and in redefining factors of production to include a broader swash of productive inputs (for example, resources, management, and technology). Defined and operationalized in these ways, it is easier to see the advantages that Norway reaped by opening to international markets. As we shall discover below, Norway benefited tremendously from importing cheaper foodstuffs and production inputs (which Norway needed) while exporting goods and services in which it enjoyed a comparative advantage.

While most economists and policy-makers today seem to agree on the mutual benefits of free trade, it would be an exaggeration to say that this has always been the case. Indeed, many development scholars remain skeptical of the benefits to poor countries from engaging in free trade. This sort of skepticism can be traced back to America's first Treasury Secretary, Alexander Hamilton. In his 1791 *Report on the Subject of Manufactures* to the US House of Representatives, Hamilton advocated the protection of nascent American industry until it could establish a strong enough footing to compete with (stronger) foreign (read British) firms. It is often forgotten that when the US was economically underdeveloped, it argued for the necessity of protecting its domestic markets from stronger, more established, foreign producers.

In the mid 1800s, this type of argument found its strongest voice in Germany. Friedrich List's (1841) *National System of Political Economy* argued that the free trade advocated by classical (British) economists was the economic policy of the strong. In other words, List held that there was no 'natural' or immutable international division of labor based on the law of comparative advantage. The existing international division of labor was merely a historical artifact resulting from prior uses of economic and political power.

As we shall discover in the chapter below, Norwegian commercial policy during this time was informed by both schools of thought. Throughout most of the period under consideration, Norwegian commercial policy was open and liberal — and this is clearly evidenced by the fact that exports and imports together represented such a large share of her GDP (see Table 5.1 below). On the whole, Norwegian policy-makers recognized the need to encourage and engage an international system of free trade.

Toward the end of the period, however, and as protectionism was rising throughout the international system, Norway began to succumb to more protectionist measures. As with many patterns in Norwegian economic history, the ups and downs of Norwegian liberalism followed closely on the tails of international norms and fashion. Still, it is important to emphasize that Norway's embrace of protectionism was almost always weaker (and later) than that of the larger states in the international system. A small state like Norway simply cannot afford to turn its back on world trade.

Norwegian commercial policy

In the first half of the 19th century, Norwegian tariff policy had remained mildly protective of the interests of the Norwegian peasantry. Larger farmers in the south and east of the country were worried about the infusion of cheaper Swedish grain. Smaller farmers along the coast were mostly self-sufficient, and saw little need to encourage imports of any type. Worse, the peasantry worried that any drop in the country's import tariffs would result in a new burden of direct taxation: a burden borne mostly by them. While merchants in Norway's nascent exporting branches (ship-owners, fish and timber exporters) leant a sympathetic ear to the doctrines of free trade, the Norwegian peasant sought moderate protectionism.

At the national level, this debate reached its fervor in the 1830s and 1840s, as parliamentarians lined up in support of either Ole Gabriel Ueland, a farmer and politician who favored protectionist policies to support domestic trade and infant industries, or Anton Martin Schweigaard, an academic and politician who led the fight for free trade. By mid century, it appeared as though Schweigaard had gotten the upper hand, as liberal economic thought was gaining support across Scandinavia. Although Norway was formally linked to Sweden during this time, it was able to develop its own commercial policy, one that was remarkably more liberal than its neighbor's.

Using a series of university lectures and articles, Professor Schweigaard was able to generate much of the support for Norway's more liberal tariff regime in the 1840s and 1850s. Indeed, T. K. Derry (1973: 107) likens Schweigaard to Richard Cobden (the indefatigable critic of Britain's Corn Laws), a likeness—as we shall see—that is not without warrant. More than anyone else, Schweigaard helped to reshape the Norwegian tariff regime in 1842 (which coincided with the first free-trade budget of Sir Robert Peel in Britain) and set Norwegian commercial policy on a more liberal course.

By mid century, and especially with the recommendations of the 1858 Tariff Commission, Norway had adopted a relatively liberal trade policy that would serve it throughout most of the remainder of the century. The resulting reduction on grain import duties reflected a new thinking about the role of agriculture in the Norwegian economy (and the expected benefits of cheap imported grains). But it also reflected a growing realization of the benefits expected from expanding markets for Norwegian fish, lumber and shipping.

This movement to freer trade was most evident in 1865, when Norway signed an agreement with France along the lines of Britain's earlier (1860) Cobden-Chevalier Treaty. With this treaty, Norway secured mutual shipping privileges, customs' reductions, and a most-favored-nations' clause that entangled her in the greater net of European trading relations. In short, Norway showed an increased willingness to grant concession to duties on foreign manufactures in return for better market access for its own exports. As this treaty lifted a number of tariffs on popular French goods (for example, glass, porcelain, paper, hats, gloves, leather, confectionery, textiles, metal goods, silk and wine), and because French demand for Norwegian goods was relatively small, it is doubtful that Norway actually won any short-term economic benefit from the treaty. Rather, Norway's gain was mostly indirect: it signaled a more internationalist engagement and the promise of greater access for its exports in international markets.

After 1865, Norwegian commercial policy became increasingly liberal. As mentioned in the previous chapter, grain duties were reduced to almost nothing in 1869, and import duties on manufactured goods were reduced significantly in 1873 (except on those manufactured commodities that could not be produced at home and which were not seen to be significant for the development of the national economy). Such a significant reduction in duties was not without cost to the Norwegian government.

After all, at the time, tariffs and duties represented the most important revenue source for the government. These revenues are represented by the large black sections of each column in Figure 5.1—a figure that lists the share of government taxes and duties over time.[1] What this figure does not show is that these revenues, in total, are increasing rather drastically over time, from just 16 million kroner in 1865 to 111 million kroner in 1914/15 (then they take-off, through the roof, during the war years)! What we do see in the figure is the dominant (if shrinking) role played by tariff revenues. In 1865, tariffs constituted 81 per cent of the central government's tax and duty incomes. Even at the end of the period, after a half century of trade liberalization, tariffs still represent almost 50 per cent of this revenue source.

At the same time, the government was actively encouraging Norwegian merchants to exploit international markets. Toward that goal, the Storting introduced a number of commercial stipends to stimulate the foreign activities of Norwegian businessmen in 1887. The money was used to arrange contacts between foreign markets and domestic producers, through a network of foreign consuls. Over time, these consuls developed from being Export Information Offices [*Oplysningsbureau for Export*] or Trade Centers [*Handelsmuseum*] to become independent trade offices (Hodne and Grytten 2000: 276). This is not inconsequential, in that Norway still did not have formal representation abroad at this time (its representation was provided by the Swedish foreign ministry as a result of the Treaty of Kiel). Thus, Norway's new trade-related consular activities

---

[1] Due to the difficulty of obtaining annual data, this table does not include another important source of government revenue at the time (income from state property, wealth and businesses). Still, this income remained relatively constant throughout the period, representing 20 per cent of all central government revenue. In addition, toward the end of the period, the central government received some transfers from the county governments, but these were generally small in size. For an overview, see Hodne (1981: 279, table 20).

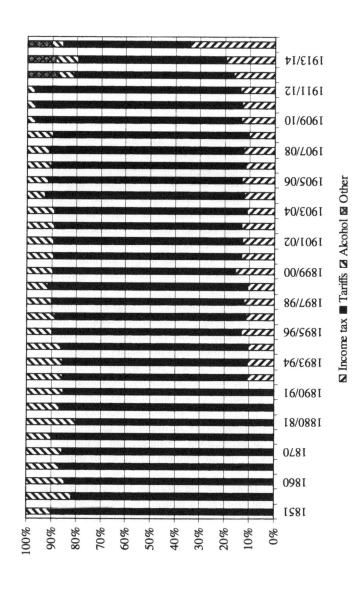

Figure 5.1   The importance of tariffs for central government revenues

Source: SSB (2000)

became the seeds of an independent Norwegian foreign service after the Union with Sweden was dissolved in 1905.

Norway's free trade posture is also very evident in its complicated trading relationship with Sweden. In 1865, the two countries maintained remarkably different tariff structures. When both countries became committed to a new, more liberal, trading regime (because of their respective treaty obligations with France), the commercial policies of the two countries needed to be streamlined. Although an 1868 proposal in the Swedish parliament [*Riksdag*] suggested the establishment of a customs' union between the two countries, the eventual (1874) legislation limited the duty-free customs' market to those commodities produced in the two countries.[2] Although this was a second-best solution for Norway, a duty-free partnership between the two countries represented a vast, if short-lived, improvement for Norwegian traders. Only eight years later, in 1888, Sweden began to raise protective barriers around her agricultural and industrial producers. As a result, Norwegian and Swedish prices began to diverge, to the benefit of Norwegian traders. By 1897 Sweden could no longer tolerate the resulting commercial hemorrhage and it terminated its common market agreement with Norway.

Sweden was just one of many countries that began to pursue a more protectionist policy. Norway was increasingly aware of the changing international attitudes to free trade and began to consider more protectionist measures in 1874, following the general international pattern outlined in Chapter 2. At that time, the Storting considered, but rejected, new statutes that would have removed all protective tariffs. From 1874 until the turn of the century, Norway began to move slowly away from its free trade principles (albeit much slower than did Sweden). Still, although moving in a protectionist direction, Norway's commercial legislation remained remarkably liberal. This is important to emphasize: while most of Europe was returning to protectionist policies, and while protectionist sentiment was increasing in Norway, the government continued to pursue a mostly liberal trading policy.

It was not until the mid 1890s that the Storting was ready to pass a tariff policy aimed at protecting nascent Norwegian industries. The repeal of the Inter-Dominion Law between Norway and Sweden in 1895 had landed a heavy blow to free trade advocates in Norway. The new tariff law of 1897 included several new duties on both manufactures and food stuffs (for example, butter and fresh meat). But the complex nature of the new customs' regime is itself evidence of the difficulty in moving away from free trade.

---

[2] Prior to this time, Norwegian-Swedish trade was subject to an Inter-Dominion Law [*mellomrikslov*] from 25 October 1815. This law granted tariff-free sales of domestic food transported on land between the two realms (and halved tariffs on sea-based trade). New legislation (in 1827) extended these benefits to almost all goods and—most importantly for Norway—it granted Norwegian ships equal rights to transport.

Aggregate view

There are two headline statistics that illustrate the important role of trade in Norway's general economic catch-up: its degree of openness and its rate of growth in trade (relative to GDP). By examining these types of aggregate statistics we get a good introduction to Norway's heavy reliance on international trade. We can then turn to a closer examination of the sorts of goods and services being exported and imported.

Norway was remarkably exposed to international markets in the late 19th century. A common indicator for international openness is the size of a nation's foreign trade (measured by combining exports and imports), as a share of GDP. By this indicator, a country is considered to be 'open' when trade constitutes more than 50 per cent of its GDP. Using this standard, the Norwegian economy was already open at the beginning of the period under study, and became increasingly so throughout the period: rising from 55.5 per cent to 69.2 per cent, with a decline in only one of the decades (around the turn of the century, when the share dropped from 63.8 to 63.3 per cent of GDP) (see Table 5.1).

Table 5.1   Exports and imports of goods and services at current prices. Moving decade averages, 1865-1914

| | Absolute figures in mill. kr. | | | Percentage shares of GDP at current prices | | | |
	Exports	Imports	Export Surplus	Exports	Imports	Openness*	Export Surplus
1865-74	166	157	+9	28.5	27.0	55.5	+1.5
1870-79	202	200	+2	28.8	28.6	57.4	+0.2
1875-84	214	214	-	28.8	28.8	57.6	-
1880-89	217	209	+8	30.3	29.1	59.4	+1.2
1885-94	226	236	-10	30.1	31.5	61.6	-1.4
1890-99	258	297	-39	29.7	34.1	63.8	-4.4
1895-04	297	346	-49	29.3	34.0	63.3	-4.7
1900-09	354	396	-42	30.5	34.0	64.5	-3.6
1905-14	490	520	-30	33.6	35.6	69.2	-2.0

*The 'Openness' column was constructed by simply adding together the percentage shares of exports and imports for every decade (in other words, the previous two columns).

Source: SSB (1966: 60, table 27)

In examining these aggregate figures a little closer, we see several remarkable trends. First of all, in the absolute figures (the first two columns in Table 5.1) we can see that the nominal value of both exports and imports increased throughout the period. (At this point it may be fruitful to point out that Norwegian domestic prices were rising faster than international prices, such that the growth in export/import volumes is even more impressive than the growth in value!)

Another trend worth noting is the fact that the value of Norway's imports in the 1880s began to exceed the value of its exports. Using the decade averages in

Table 5.1, we see that exports and imports each represented close to a third of the total GDP during most of the period after 1865. By 1905 the export sector had even passed beyond this level. This general upward trend was punctuated by three decades of retarded growth or stagnation (1875-1884; 1885-1894, indicative of the general stagnation in the international economy; and again in 1895-1905). If we measure using 1938 prices, we find that imports and exports amounted to just over 15 per cent of GDP in 1865-1874, as against 26 per cent and 23 per cent in 1905-1914 (SSB 1966: 57, table 26). On the other hand, measured at current prices, as in Table 5.1, the GDP shares of imports and exports increased much less. This means that the price of imports and exports must have declined compared to the prices for total production.

As a result, Norway began to suffer an increasingly large trade deficit with the outside world. Briefly, Norway's annual growth rates for the period from 1865 to 1900 were: GDP (1.9); exports (2.3); and imports (3.8). Clearly, the growth in Norwegian imports was faster than the growth of either its exports or GDP. By the turn of the century this trade deficit was close to 50 million kroner (or nearly five per cent of GDP), before dropping again in the early 1900s. This deficit need not be a problem, if used to secure necessary services and goods. Like a young family planning to grow, it can be desirable for a national economy to borrow against future growth. As we shall see below, this seems to have been the case in Norway.

A second important observation concerns trade's rate of growth, relative to GDP. Table 5.1 shows how Norwegian economic growth depended critically on exports in the latter part of the 19th century: Norwegian exports, as a share of GDP, increased until the turn of the century (peaking at 30.3 per cent), fell for a couple of decades (down to 29.3 per cent of GDP), then increased again prior to World War I. The fact that exports were growing faster than GDP for most of this period provides a strong indication that Norwegian economic growth was export-driven.

The balance between Norwegian imports and exports was also quite uneven over time. Compared to the growth in Norway's volume of imports, Norwegian exports grew relatively slowly before the turn of the century. The strongest period of import growth was in the 1870s and the mid 1880s, as the prices of imports were falling relative to the domestic price level. Not surprisingly, the volume of imports at the time grew significantly stronger than the country's GDP (SSB 1966: 58). In the 1900s, however, the tables turned, and export growth surpassed import growth.

Finally, we might note that most of Norway's trade at the time was bilateral—its focus was on a few, very important, trading partners. When we exclude shipping revenues, most of Norwegian exports (about 42 per cent) and a good share of its imports (about 29 per cent) were with Great Britain at the turn of the century. Norway's next biggest trading partner was Germany, which was responsible for 14 per cent of Norway's exports and 28 per cent of her imports. From these countries Norway imported the essential machines and industrial inputs that powered her economic catch-up. After Great Britain and Germany, Norway's third largest trading partner was Sweden, which was responsible for ten per cent of Norway's exports and ten per cent of her imports.

At the turn of the century, Norway also traded with other countries, but at lower levels. Norway had trade deficits with Russia (three per cent of exports; eight per cent of imports) and the United States (0.5 per cent of exports; six per cent imports), a trade surplus with Spain (seven per cent of exports; one per cent of imports) and rough trade balances with Denmark, the Netherlands and Belgium (about four to five per cent of both imports and exports) (Hodne and Grytten 1992: 49).

Export composition

As with the GDP figures examined in the previous chapter, the aggregate trade figures tend to conceal much about the changing nature of Norwegian exports. Table 5.2 interrogates these aggregate figures to reveal three important trends in Norwegian exports during this time.

The first important trend to note is that Norway's foreign earnings at the time were mostly generated by the Norwegian shipping fleet. Although there is some variation over the period, roughly 40 per cent of Norway's foreign revenues came from its ocean freight earnings. It would seem that shipping, more than any other economic activity, paid for Norway's heavy reliance on imports.

Table 5.2   Composition of exports at current prices. Percentage figures, selected years

	1865	1875	1885	1895	1905	1915
Fish, whale-oil & other products from hunting	21.8	20.1	16.4	17.4	15.6	14.6
Timber, wood, pulp, paper & paper products	23.6	19.0	19.7	20.4	21.9	14.0
Products from mining; metals & chemical products	2.9	3.3	3.2	2.4	3.4	11.7
Other industrial products	5.3	6.7	9.2	11.0	9.7	13.7
Gross freight earnings by ocean Shipping	41.4	45.2	43.3	38.9	32.5	39.9
Other exports	5.0	5.7	8.2	9.9	16.9	6.1
Total exports of goods & services	100.0	100.0	100.0	100.0	100.0	100.0

Source: SSB (1966: 64, table 30)

Norwegian ships tended to specialize in three types of transport. Most significantly, Norway specialized in the tramp trade of lumber. Indeed, about 70 per cent of Norwegian freight in 1880 occurred between foreign harbors, and the majority of this trade (about 56 per cent) was in lumber (Hodne 1981: 144). But Norwegian ship-owners were also pioneers in the transport of oil, and were heavily involved in emigrant traffic (although not in the permanent Liner traffic). As the (dominant) timber transport tended to rely on slow and inefficient (but large) sailing vessels, there was little incentive to modernize the fleet. This, in part, explains Norway's tardy (and costly) transition to iron and steam, as described in Chapter 4 (note also the decline in shipping's relative export earnings between 1885 and 1895).

The second observation is familiar, as we dwelled on it in the previous chapter. In particular, a very significant share of Norwegian export earnings (that are not related to shipping) is found in the export of traditional (primary) goods. If we combine the first two rows in Table 5.2 to construct a rough indicator of primary exports,[3] we see that primary export revenues are almost as large as shipping revenues: just under 40 per cent and falling throughout the period (except in 1865, where they were the largest, totaling 45.4 per cent).

Finally, two categories of exports were increasing their share over the period: various mining, metal and chemical products—which jumped phenomenally in 1915—and other industrial products (which included, among other things, products from the oil and fat industry). The category 'mining; metal and chemical exports' is made up of those new export products from the likes of *Norsk Hydro* (for example, aluminum, zinc, nickel, calcium carbide, ferroalloys and, especially 'Norwegian saltpeter') that we read about in the previous chapter. From 1905 to 1915, the export share of this category rose from 3.4 per cent to a remarkable 11.7 per cent (see Table 5.2). While these new industrial products were increasing their share of export value over most of the period, they still remained small compared to the foreign revenues generated by trade in the shipping and primary exports' markets.

The final row in Table 5.2, 'other exports', includes the export of a variety of different agricultural products, non-shipping services, used ships, and so on. Most interesting of these, to my mind, is the export of ice. Of course, ice is very heavy. Still, ice represented three per cent of Norwegian net shipping tonnage (at 109,000 tons) in 1879 (Hodne 1981: 44). Indeed, the foreign demand for ice was climbing along with standards of living in Europe, and Norway sat atop a mountainous supply of ice-covered water and glaciers. There can be little debating the fact that Norway enjoys an abundance of ice. Unoccupied farmers and sailors were able to beef up their meager incomes by cutting ice from frozen lakes in the eastern and southern part of the country, or by harvesting glaciers along the coast (where it was possible to get ice in the summer). The first mention of Norwegian ice exports was in 1847 (when 332 tons were shipped), but by 1898 Norway was exporting 554,000 tons to London, Glasgow, Dieppe, Boulogne and other European cities (Hodne and Grytten 2000: 275).

Table 5.2 helps us to put Norway's industrial development in check. As we saw in the previous chapter, Norway did undergo a significant industrial

---

[3] This is somewhat problematic, as we learned in the last chapter—many of the timber-related products are industrial products. Thus, this combined indicator is not a pristine measure of primary products' exports.

transformation at the close of the 19th century. But these changes were not yet making any sort of major impact on Norwegian export revenues. For most of the period, about 80 per cent of Norway's foreign revenues were still being generated by the country's traditional export sectors (such as fishing, whaling, timber and shipping). Norway remained heavily dependent on a natural resource-based economy, albeit one that was becoming more efficient and productive over time.

Import composition

We have already discussed the important role played by the arrival of cheap international grain in Norway's economic transformation. By lifting tariffs on most foodstuffs, Norwegians were able to purchase foreign grain for much cheaper than if they had produced it at home. This, in turn, forced Norwegian farmers to search for alternative niches (such as animal husbandry), to adopt more productive measures, or to leave farming altogether.

Thus, from 1850 to 1900, food stuffs were the dominant Norwegian import. In terms of value, the most important import items were grain, meat, pork, butter, coffee, and sugar. To give the reader an impression of how important the food trade was, Hodne and Grytten (2000: 98) note that grain and flour imports represented 38 per cent of all the imports offloaded in Bergen's harbor in 1880. Food imports were followed in importance by the import of inputs for Norwegian handicrafts and industrial production, such as cotton, flax, hemp, iron (both raw and bar), steel, coal, machines, paper, petroleum and ships (Hodne and Grytten 1992: 48-9).

Even after the turn of the century (1900-1904), the import of grain and grain goods topped the list of Norwegian imports (at 18 per cent); followed by minerals, especially coal and coke (13 per cent); manufactures such as yarn, cloth and ready made clothing (eight per cent); grocer goods such as coffee, sugar, tea, tobacco, spices and cocoa (eight per cent); and ships, carriages and machines (seven per cent) (Hodne and Grytten 1992: 49).

Given Norway's climate and landscape, it is not remarkable or surprising that it needed to import so much of its grain and grocer needs. What is more noteworthy, however, is the sizeable import of items that were used as inputs for production (and subsequent export). Indeed, while the export composition figures did not reveal much significance to Norway's nascent industrial activity, the import composition figures do.

Between 1851 and 1913, Norwegian imports multiplied thirteen fold. While grain and food imports remained important, their share of total Norwegian imports was dropping through the period. This is evident in Table 5.3 below, where we see that the import of consumption goods in Norway actually dropped from 35.2 per cent in 1865 to just 24.9 per cent in 1915. In short, the growth in Norwegian imports during this period was not in the form of unnecessary consumption items.

Indeed, over half of all imports between 1865 and 1905 were used as goods and services' inputs for Norwegian production. In addition, another seven to

Norwegian Catch-Up

ten per cent of Norwegian imports took the form of investment or investment goods (see Table 5.3). As the Norwegian economy was beginning to take-off, and at a time when we might expect to see a rapid increase in demand for the import of finished (consumer) products, we see that Norway continues to import mostly goods used in domestic production (for example, metal in raw form, coal from England, mineral salt, and lighting oil).

Consider, for example, Norway's production and export of calcium carbide (described briefly in the previous chapter). While Norway enjoyed an abundance of the main inputs for this production (cheap electricity and high-grade limestone), it lacked the necessary steel to finish the export package, as finished calcium carbide was packed and shipped in steel drums. Thus, in order to export carbides, Norway had to first import steel sheets for the manufacture of the packing drums.

Table 5.3   Composition of imports at current prices. Percentage figures, selected years

	1865	1875	1885	1895	1905	1915
Consumer goods & services	35.2	37.9	36.3	37.1	30.8	24.9
Investment goods	7.7	8.6	6.6	10.3	8.7	12.8
Goods & services for input in Norwegian production	56.4	52.3	55.2	49.6	53.3	60.7
Of which						
• Goods for input in the construction sector	2.8	4.1	2.8	3.6	3.8	6.4
• Operating costs abroad by ocean shipping & whaling	9.2	11.1	12.3	10.3	8.9	9.2
• Other goods & services for input in Norwegian production	44.4	37.1	40.1	35.7	40.6	45.1
Re-export	0.7	1.2	1.9	3.0	7.2	1.6
Total imports of goods & services, incl. customs' duties	100.0	100.0	100.0	100.0	100.0	100.0

Source: SSB (1966: 65, table 31)

Despite Norway's growing appetite for imports, these statistics reveal a fairly appealing set of circumstances for an underdeveloped economy. Norway's relative poverty in many critical goods (such as foodstuffs) and her demand for essential input items were now being met by world suppliers. These inputs could then be fused with what Norway brought to international tables of trade: an abundance of natural resources (such as fish, timber and hydroelectric power). Better yet, the trade imbalance that resulted from this heavy reliance on imports could be paid for with the revenues generated by Norway's merchant fleet.

Conclusion

Norwegian economic catch-up relied heavily on an export-driven growth model. The first step in exploiting this model is in realizing the value of letting Norway become less self-sufficient in the production of its grain and food needs. By dropping tariffs on grain and foodstuffs, Norwegians enjoyed access to cheaper food than was available domestically. As we saw in the last chapter, the resulting shock to local producers encouraged them to develop new production niches (for example, animal husbandry), more efficient techniques, or to leave farming all together. This, in turn, freed up much labor for employment in the new, more productive, and growing industrial sectors.

More significant was the international demand for goods that required vast amounts of electricity for their production. Given this demand, Norway found itself attractive to foreign investors who could import the capital, skills and technology that was necessary to exploit Norway's hydroelectric potential. This provided economies of scale that were unavailable in the domestic market. Technological developments and market access also breathed new life into traditional Norwegian export sectors such as fishing, timber and shipping.

Finally, international trade not only benefited Norwegian producers and consumers, but it was also critical for the survival of the most important foreign revenue generator in the Norwegian economy: its shipping fleet. The fate of the Norwegian shipping industry ebbed and flowed with the tide of global trade.

In short, Norway's economic catch-up depended critically on its access to international markets. But to fully exploit these markets, Norway needed access to investment capital, which it dearly lacked. Like Norway's dependence on foreign goods and service markets, Norwegian catch-up relied heavily on foreign capital markets. This is the subject of the chapter that follows.

Conclusion

Chapter 6

Capital Gains

It is difficult to imagine Norway's remarkable economic expansion in the absence of foreign financing. After all, many of Norway's most important industrial exports, as described in the last chapter, were funded by foreigners. Developing and exporting these new products required significant amounts of fresh, relatively risk-averse, capital. Yet in Norway at the time, the domestic capital market was not sufficiently mature to provide for this need. In the absence of a mature domestic capital market, Norway relied heavily on international lenders to spark its economic and industrial transformation.

Of course, an over-reliance on foreign financing can introduce as many problems as it solves. This is especially true for a young country, like Norway, which was struggling for her own political independence at the time. Consequently, the Norwegian authorities were forced to balance a fine line between welcoming the international finance that was essential for her future prosperity and growth, and curtailing its influence on a young and impressionable nation state.

Recognizing this dilemma, Norway's reliance on international finance was neither blind nor complete. Most importantly, government regulation—especially the concession laws—severely limited the political and economic influence of foreign investors in Norway. In this way Norway's economic dependence on international lenders did not translate into direct political control. At the same time, it is important to emphasize that the lion's share of capital available for the general economy came from domestic sources. International finance was channeled into the largest, the most capital intensive, the most productive and the most export-oriented industries. It is not a coincidence that these industries were also the most profitable. In this way, a maturing domestic capital market had to focus its relatively meager resources on the country's more traditional credit needs.

To examine this complex relationship between the nascent Norwegian industrial economy and its foreign financiers, I have divided this chapter into three sections. The first section provides a short introduction to the role of capital markets (both domestic and international) in modern economic theory. I then sketch a picture of the changing nature of Norway's domestic capital markets at this time. After all, Norway's reliance on foreign capital is, in large part, a reflection of the shortcomings of its own (domestic) capital market. The third section then examines Norway's reliance on international capital by focusing on foreign direct investments.

Capital ideas

Any industrial transformation requires access to capital for investment. Indeed, for many development economists, significant capital formation is the crucial component for development. In larger countries, this investment capital usually comes from the generation of economic surplus, stored as savings. Stereotypically, this surplus was generated in the large landed estates of feudal Europe, where the manor lord could not manage to spend his surplus on consumption items. Rather than letting this surplus gather dust under his bed, the lord lent it out in return for a small fee. It is in this way that we have come to think of the rise of the European bourgeoisie.

Of course, Norway lacked large feudal estates and the surpluses that they might have generated. Consequently, Norway never developed the capital, class, or traditions associated with a strong and independent class of financiers. Indeed, many would have it that Norway was absolutely puritan in its condemnation of surplus. This puritan attitude is clearly depicted in the popular Danish film rendition of *Babette's Feast*, based on a novel by Isak Dinesen (Karen Blixen) about life in a tiny Norwegian coastal town at the end of the 19th century. In Blixen's novel, and the film adaptation, even life's simplest pleasures are condemned and avoided. Norwegian mores and legislation, even to the present day, reflect this traditional disdain for surplus and profit.

While moralists may applaud this attitude toward surplus and pleasure, it is abhorred by economists as a distinct handicap. This handicap became all the more menacing as industrial development requires access to larger and larger pools of investment capital. After all, it is not easy to build a hydroelectric dam from money stored under the mattress.

Norway is not particularly unique in this regard. Many developing countries lack sufficient resources to finance their investment needs. To meet these needs, developing countries must depend on international capital markets in three distinct forms: the authorities (central and local government, or large firms) can float bonds in international financial centers, they can try and attract direct foreign investors, or they can draw on more personal sources of foreign finance in the form of remittances. All three of these financial strategies remain viable. In addition, however, today's developing economies can borrow from large international agencies such as the World Bank and International Monetary Fund.

The economic logic of foreign borrowing is quite similar to that driving foreign trade, as described in the previous chapter. Standard economic theory would have it that foreign capital inflows unambiguously increase the rate of investment in developing countries. The argument is not difficult to follow: savings are abundant in the developed world. (The developed world is, after all, rich.) As a result, the returns on investments there are relatively low, because the amount of capital per worker is already high. This follows from a basic economic truism: that the price of a good (even capital) depends on supply and demand. When capital is abundant, its price (or rate of return) will be lower.

In developing countries, on the other hand, returns on investments are relatively high as the amount of capital per worker is comparatively low. The relative absence of capital in the developing world should ensure it a higher price (return). Hence, in theory, there is a clear incentive for capital to move across national frontiers, from the developed to the developing world, in search of higher returns. Consequently, international capital mobility should help poorer nations to achieve faster growth and thus promote economic convergence among nations.

This is the economic logic of convergence associated with the work of Robert Solow. Global factor mobility should allow developing countries access to the capital they need for economic growth and catch-up. In theory, access to international finance should favor poor countries, as capital will flow from rich to poor countries and create a higher rate of growth in the backward economy (while the rate of growth in capital-rich states slows down). In this way, many economists believe that the incomes of poor countries will converge eventually with those of the rich.

In practice, however, this convergence does not seem to occur very often. Income differentials across countries have actually grown over time, despite increased capital market integration. While world per capita incomes in the 1820s were relatively similar (and low), they began to diverge significantly with Europe's industrialization and the economic growth that it generated (World Bank 2000: 45ff). Indeed, one of the most animated debates in contemporary economics is about whether globalization actually generates income divergence across (and within) countries. In the context of this debate, the Norwegian experience in the late 19th century is an anomaly of great interest. The Norwegian catch-up is an example of economic practice actually coinciding with economic theory! The question for students of economic development is clear: what is so special or unique about the Norwegian case?

This book is an attempt to answer that difficult question. An important part of that answer, I think, lies in Norway's relationship to international capital markets. There can be little question that Norway benefited greatly from its access to international finance, but to understand Norway' reliance on, and relationship to, foreign sources of capital, we must first understand the nature and shortcomings of Norway's domestic capital market.

The domestic market for capital

The Norwegian domestic market for capital was always underdeveloped. There are several reasons for this, including the structural limitations of the Norwegian economy, cultural attitudes of Norwegians to economic surplus, prior dependence on Danish and Swedish financiers and entrepreneurs, and even domestic legislation that limited the potential of a nascent banking industry. Before we can come to grips with Norway's reliance on foreign sources of capital, we need to take a closer look at these unique characteristics of her domestic credit market.

We have already learned that Norway was a poor country, generating little if any significant agricultural surplus. Savings and investments were a luxury that most Norwegians simply could not afford. In many ways, this basic condition underlies the others: it helps to explain Norwegian attitudes to accumulation and surplus and the (related) legislation that constrained a nascent Norwegian banking sector. As an example of the latter, banks faced several restrictions on their ability to privately issue bearer bonds (until 1897), and Norway did not even have a law regulating equity markets until 1910.[1] Consequently, Norway's access to domestic capital was limited.

This relative scarcity of domestic capital can be illustrated by two comparative measures. First of all, Norwegian interest rates were relatively high during this time. In particular, the average discount rate between 1846 and 1877 was higher in Norway (5.13 per cent) than it was in any of its neighbors and most important trading partners (for example, England (3.93 per cent); France (4.13 per cent); Germany (4.46 per cent); Denmark (4.54 per cent); and Sweden (5.07 per cent) (Hodne 1981: 402). As interest rates are simply the price of capital, and the price of something (such as capital) is determined largely by supply and demand, the higher interest rate can be seen as an indicator of the relative scarcity of Norwegian capital at the time.

Another indication of the relative scarcity of Norwegian capital can be seen by comparing its volume of credit relative to GDP, as is done in Table 6.1. With these figures it is important to emphasize that the total credit volume (in column 1) captures both foreign and domestic credit—so Table 6.1 illustrates Norway's supply of credit from all sources. Here we see that the Norwegian credit volume really took off at the turn of the century, both in nominal and per GDP terms. Indeed, after 1905, the Norwegian credit volume (1,230 million kr) exceeded its GDP (1,106 million kr)!

On the surface, this lending quota (in other words, the volume of credit divided by GDP) appears impressive. The Norwegian economy was getting access to a growing supply of credit for its expansion needs. Much of this supply, as we shall see below, comes from abroad—and the increasing lending quota illustrates this growing role played by foreign capital in Norway. But when we compare these trends with those in Denmark (a country similar in terms of population and GDP), we get a more nuanced picture of the underdeveloped nature of Norwegian capital markets. While the credit volume in Denmark increased fourteen-fold over this period, it only increased nine-fold in Norway. At the end of the period, in 1913, Norway's lending quota was 113 per cent, whereas Denmark enjoyed a lending quota of 159 per cent. Compared to Denmark, Norway was not generating sufficient credit at a critical period of economic transformation. This evidence lends support to the claims made by several of Norway's influential early economists (for example, Wilhelm Keilhau): the Norwegian savings rate in 1900 was too low to finance her industrialization (Hodne 1981: 408).

---

[1] Although there was a law for joint stock companies from 1848, and a new general law was passed in 1895, its first Companies Act [*aksjelov*] came in 1910 (Hodne 1981: 401).

Table 6.1   Volume of credit, relative to GDP

	Credit volume (1), in mill. kr	GDP (2), in mill. kr	Lending quota (1:2), in %
1865	227	480	47
1870	259	542	48
1875	361	771	47
1880	407	720	57
1885	494	679	73
1890	594	780	76
1895	704	832	85
1900	1,083	1,115	97
1905	1,230	1,106	111
1910	1,666	1,435	116
1913	2,093	1,854	113

Source: Hodne (1981: 407)

To compensate for this shortage of capital, especially in the earliest years of our study, the Norwegian government played an active role in securing foreign capital. In addition to its various development projects (such as building railroads and telegraph networks), the government provided most of the financing for early Norwegian development. The bulk of this activity was channeled through a network of small credit outlets run by the Department of Finance [*diskonteringskommisjoner*], the central bank, and eventually through a specialized Mortgage Bank, all of which funded their activities by floating bonds in international financial centers.

In the first half of the 19th century, the central bank was one of the most important sources of finance (outside the family and community, *ala* the *partsrederiet* as described in Chapter 4). Established in 1816, Norges Bank had two central functions: to ensure the external value of the Norwegian currency vis-à-vis other currencies and to supply the economy with a sufficient supply of money (or liquidity).

The first objective was secured by linking the Norwegian currency to a stable external anchor. In particular, Norway maintained an effective silver standard from 1842 until 1875 and a gold standard from 1875 until 1914. The latter was a function of membership in a larger common currency union with Sweden and Denmark. As described in Chapter 2, many European states were already following Britain's lead in adopting a gold standard. Sparked by falling international prices and business confidence, the Scandinavian countries followed suit by forming their own currency union, the Scandinavian Currency Union, which Norway joined in 1875/77 (some years after Sweden and Denmark). The krone was minted independently in each country (but was legal tender in all of them) and was given a fixed value in gold, slightly above the English Victorian shilling. This solution cushioned each currency from the full effects of the fall in international prices (which continued from the mid 1870s to the mid 1890s).

This practice of providing a rigid external anchor assured the free convertibility of the Norwegian currency, which—in turn—facilitated international trade. To ensure the autonomy and independence of the central bank, the authorities placed its headquarters in Trondheim, keeping it far from the meddling hands of the authorities and business community.[2]

The central bank also played an important role in regulating the amount of domestic liquidity, or capital in circulation. Norges Bank was the dominant domestic lender for most of the earlier period, and it was a conservative one in that it focused on long-term loans and required collateral in property. Indeed, in the 1830s, around 90 per cent of its loan collateral was in the form of property! In addition, the central bank enjoyed a monopoly on the issue of currency notes, which—in turn—probably retarded the Norwegian banking sector. While it is common today for a central bank to enjoy this monopoly, it was not so in the late 19th century. Sweden, for example, had 27 note-issuing banks in 1890 (Hodne 1981: 394). As a result of this monopoly, the nascent Norwegian banking sector was shielded from an important source of potential revenue as well as the experience and international contacts that note-issuing brought.

By mid century the government had come to realize the problem of relying too heavily on the central bank. The agricultural sector, in particular, was in dire need of new capital on better terms. The state response was the 1851 establishment of the Mortgage Bank [*Kongeriket Norges Hypotekbank*], which helped farmers get access to capital by giving long-term loans on agricultural land at low rates of interest. It also allowed the state to reduce its long-term lending with collateral in property, and focus more on short-term commercial loans. Using the state as guarantor, the Hypotekbank floated bonds in Copenhagen and Hamburg, then later in Paris (1899), Berlin (1907) and London (1914). While the bank's focus was at first in the southern and eastern districts, it came to extend its activity throughout Norway. Indeed, by 1910, the bank held almost 20 per cent of all Norwegian farmers' long-term debt (Hodne and Grytten 2000: 160).

In short, the Norwegian state was remarkably active in international financial markets at the time, and it was the most important provider of domestic capital. This high level of state involvement reflected the fact that a significant commercial bank sector did not develop until the middle of the 19th century, and that the broader Norwegian banking sector did not exert itself and develop international contacts of its own until the end of the century.

The Norwegian private bank market was surprisingly small and tardy in its development. Norway's first savings bank was established in 1822 (*Christiania Sparebank*) and by 1840 there were 26 of them spread across the country. Most of these savings banks aimed to meet the small saver's need for small investments— they were not really designed to facilitate social investment.

---

[2] The main headquarters of Norges Bank stayed in Trondheim from 1816 until 1897. This is rather remarkable in that news traveled slowly at the time. Before 1857, when a telegraph line finally connected the two cities, Trondheim remained six postal days away from the capital city, the country's largest financial market!

Around mid century things began to change when the country's first commercial bank (*Christiania Kreditkasse*) was established (in 1848). Over the next ten years, five other commercial banks followed suit. By 1860, these commercial banks had established themselves as an important source of domestic capital, as they were already lending more money than the savings banks had in 1850 (Bergh et al. 1983: 193). Indeed, as a result of the rise in commercial banking, the volume of loans increased six-fold between 1875 and 1914 (Hovland 1995: 288). Still, Norway never developed the large solid investment banks that could play the role of entrepreneurs (as in Germany), and Norwegian banks were seldom involved in starting new companies.

By 1895 the international economy was expanding rapidly, and this gave rise to new possibilities in the development of Norway's export sector. As a result, the Norwegian credit market went through a radical transformation: commercial banks expanded their activity substantially, and a national credit system began to develop and expand beyond its self-imposed exile in the cities. State lending decreased in relative terms, as local credit institutions began to pop up across the country to provide capital. Concomitantly, a real stock market developed, and its number of trades increased rapidly.

The impetus for international capital was not just in the form of increased demand for Norwegian exports. Indeed, it might be said that a number of coincidental circumstances collided to explain Norway's heavy reliance on foreign capital. By the end of the century it seemed as though a domestic capital market was beginning to develop before being soaked in the burst of a speculative bubble. In the late 1890s, Christiania (later called Oslo) was experiencing an enormous property boom, which ended with a spectacular crash in 1899.[3] The effect on Norwegian equity and property prices was devastating. In fact, it has been said that the Norwegian equities markets were as good as dead for the first five to six years after the crash (Bergh et al. 1983: 206). As this crisis occurred at a time when the international economy was still expanding, Norwegian entrepreneurs found it easy and necessary to access other (more international) sources of finance.

As a result, much of the industrial growth described in Chapter 4 was financed by foreign direct investors: in 1909 foreigners provided 115 of the 295 million kroner (or about 39 per cent) invested in Norwegian industry (Hodne 1981: 406). But if we extend our glance beyond the industrial sector, it is possible to see the influence of a maturing domestic capital market in Norway. After all, in 1909 the Norwegian capital stock [*aksjekapital*] totaled 695 million kroner (as compared to an industrial capital stock of just 295 million kroner). Using this larger figure,

---

[3] Popular history has it that the crash started when a young messenger boy had overheard one of the most important financiers in the capital say that this was the last time he could pay all of his creditors. The boy's next delivery was to another large business, where he relayed the information. Panic set in, and a chain reaction ensued. Credit was withdrawn from the first company (despite the chairman's protests that the original news had been incorrect) and the bank supporting him was forced to close. Other companies got news of this and began to act in accordance with the rumors.

foreign capital represented a rather modest 16.5 per cent. The same trend can be seen in the employment figures. Although foreign firms were employing 13.6 per cent of the total industrial labor force in 1909, this represented only 2.6 per cent of Norway's economically active population (Stonehill 1965: 32).

To conclude, I do not wish to minimize the growing potential of the Norwegian domestic credit market. This market was providing an important source of investment for the broader Norwegian economy. Only in the industrial sector, where the capital needs were larger and more risky, did foreign financing play a significant role. But in addressing this important need, foreign capital freed up its domestic counterpart so that it could address the broader needs of the Norwegian economy.

Foreign sources

Norway relied on three channels to access foreign capital: international lending in the form of bonds floated in international financial centers, the capital that came from migrants (either in the form of remittances or in the pockets of returning migrants) and foreign direct investment. For a number of reasons, it is not possible to give equal weight to these three sources. First of all, they were not equally important in terms of size and influence, although they satisfied different needs within the Norwegian economy. Second, these sources of finance are not equally easy to trace; personal remittances, in particular, are very difficult to follow. Finally, the Norwegian government tended to welcome foreign portfolio lending and remittances, but was very leery of the political consequences of foreign direct investors.

This section will focus on the role of foreign direct investment as a source for funding Norway's nascent industrialization. This focus results from the fact that most previous research has been done in this area (as a consequence, it is difficult to get dependable accounts of remittance flows and foreign borrowing). But it is also in this area that the state was most active in channeling resources in a way that was politically tenable for a young state that was establishing its independence. In short, by looking at how Norway managed its reliance on foreign direct investment we learn an important lesson about the sort of political latitude a state could enjoy during this period of globalization.

Despite this considerable political meddling, the flow of foreign direct investment into Norway was large and significant. In 1913, foreign equity capital in Norwegian companies was about 300 million kroner. While this is an impressive amount (and we will examine its content below), it represents just a little more than half of the amount of public debt (570 million kroner) held in foreign hands. In addition, private companies had a number of special lending accounts and short-term credit arrangements; so that Norway's total foreign debt was at least 900 million kroner, or over 50 per cent of GDP (Bergh et al. 1983: 207). In other words, most of Norwegian foreign lending came by way of official and private borrowing abroad, and most of this activity occurred around the turn of the century.

This sort of indebtedness can cause serious problems for developing countries, as witnessed today by a growing movement for international 'debt forgiveness'. In this respect, Norway was extremely lucky: World War I and economic growth eventually consumed her substantial foreign debt. A neutral country, Norway made its own killing by shipping goods for warring powers: by 1919, she had become a creditor nation—probably for the first time in her history.

Between 1840 and 1870 the government hardly changed its net position, and its borrowing from abroad was rather insignificant. Then, in the final three decades of the century, the situation changed rather remarkably: Norway experienced considerable net borrowing from abroad, by both private and government sectors. Between 1870-1890 foreigners accounted for nearly a third of the total increase in debt in the Norwegian sectors of which we are aware. The largest part of this was debt accrued to the state.

The main object of government borrowing was railway construction, but (as we saw above) foreign borrowing was also used to fund the lending activities of its Hypotekbank. Norwegian railways were built in the 1870s with state bonds held abroad (first in Denmark and Germany, later in the French market, carried by large Swedish banks). Norway began to amass large debts abroad, with state officials (at a variety of levels) being important middle-men (Bergh et al. 1983: 158). Foreign debt on the public account rose precipitously: from 40 million in 1874 to 120 million in 1890 to 361 million kroner in 1900. Of the latter figure (361 million), 219 million kroner of the debt were in the form of Norwegian government bonds, 90 million were Hypotekbanken's bonds and 52 million were held in municipal bonds (Stonehill 1965: 18). By 1913, foreign holdings of Norwegian securities totaled over 868 million kroner, 300 of which were held in Norwegian private enterprises and the remainder was divided between government bonds (national and municipal) and public bank (for example, Hypotekbanken) bonds (Stonehill 1965: 20). It is quite possible that Norway imported as much as a billion kroner between 1895 and 1914 (SSB 1966).

In Table 6.2, we begin to see the impact of capital imports in Norway around 1890. The author of these statistics, Juul Bjerke, warns us of their fickleness, so we will treat them with caution (SSB 1966: 66-67). Still, the general pattern in the data reveals the same pattern described in the text: before 1890, Norway's foreign account remained more or less in balance, and some decade averages even enjoyed a surplus. After 1890, however, Norway's balance of payments' deficit begins to take a nose dive, in terms of both GDP and gross domestic capital formation. Indeed, for the decades around 1900 this foreign capital constituted about a third of Norway's gross capital formation!

In the midst of all this foreign activity, around 1909, the Norwegian statistical bureau (SSB) conducted a poll of industrial ownership. This poll provides us with a snapshot of the influence of foreign capital at that time. As Table 6.2 suggests, about a third of the total capital investments in 1909 were foreign, but we also know that there were thirty two wholly foreign corporations operating in Norway at the time.

The 1909 industrial ownership survey revealed that foreign owners contributed some 115 million kroner, or about 39 per cent of the country's equity capital in the nation's industrial joint stock companies. Of course, it is important to remember that only a small portion of Norwegian production was organized as joint stock companies at the time. Still, foreign capital was responsible for financing the most advanced companies in the electrochemical, electrometallurgical, paper and mining industries.

Table 6.2　Surplus (+) and deficit (-) in Norway's balance of payments. Moving decade averages

	Million kr	% of GDP	% of Gross domestic capital formation
1865-1874	+7	+1.2	+8.4
1870-1879	-2	-0.2	-1.8
1875-1884	-5	-0.7	-4.2
1880-1889	+3	+0.5	+2.8
1885-1894	-16	-2.2	-13.5
1890-1899	-46	-5.1	-30.1
1895-1904	-59	-5.6	-33.2
1900-1909	-59	-5.0	-29.0
1905-1914	-46	-3.1	-16.2

Source: SSB (1966: 67, table 32)

The poll also revealed that the distribution of this foreign direct investment varied significantly from sector to sector. Over 92 per cent of the foreign-held capital stock was located in four export sectors: chemicals, paper (pulp), electricity and mining (Stonehill 1965: 33-35). Table 6.3 lists the foreign capital share of Norwegian industry by branch. In the chemicals' industry, for example, 85 per cent of the total capital stock was in foreign hands (either in foreign-owned firms, or in joint—Norwegian and foreign—firms).

Table 6.3　Distribution of capital stock by type of activity and owner as of 31 December 1909

Branch	Total capital (million kr)	Foreign capital (million kr)	Foreign capital (as % of total)
Mines	31.1	25.0	80.3
Metal	7.0	2.3	32.5
Chemicals	47.1	40.0	85.0
Heat and light	20.8	9.7	46.7
Textiles	14.7	1.2	8.1
Paper, leather & rubber	72.4	32.1	44.3
Others	101.7	4.2	4.1
Total	294.8	114.5	38.8

Source: Jörberg (1973: 434).

A strong foreign influence, with deep roots, is most obvious in the mining sector. As early as 1870, more than half of the Norwegian mining industry was owned by foreigners (Jörberg 1973: 431). By the 1909 industrial poll, foreign interests (mostly Swedish and British) controlled almost the entire Norwegian mining industry. Indeed, of the 22 registered mining establishments, only one small corporation depended solely on Norwegian capital. In total, foreigners held 80.3 per cent of the total capital stock in the mining industry—most of this influence was in the form of joint stock corporations, where foreign interests were dominant (Stonehill 1965: 38).

This foreign influence included one of the most important Norwegian mining companies, *Sulitjelma Aktiegruber*, which was founded in 1891 by Swedish investors. Of the three biggest pyrite mines in Norway, two were Swedish and one was British; other ore enterprises at different times attracted German, French, and even Belgian capital (Derry 1973: 197). This heavy reliance on foreign financing is not surprising, if only because up-to-date mining equipment was expensive, and the profits produced were uncertain.

The Norwegian timber industry also relied on foreign financing as interest grew in Norway's potential to generate cheap water power (and in the industries that relied on that cheap power). The British were especially keen on owning the upstream supply for its growing pulp industry, as fully-owned subsidiaries abroad were used to limit the cost and influence of independent foreign suppliers. Accordingly, the two main operators in Norway in the 1890s were foreign owned and controlled. In 1892, *Edward Lloyd Ltd*, a large British paper concern, took over *Hønnefoss Brug* and expanded its production capacity to become the largest in Norway at the time (Stonehill 1965: 31). Similarly, in 1899 the *Kellner-Partington Paper Pulp Company Ltd* was founded with British capital for the purpose of buying the Borregaard estate at Tune. This was one of the most important of the early foreign investments and it soon became the largest Norwegian producer of mechanical and chemical pulp.

Norway's reliance on foreign capital is perhaps most noticeable in the hydroelectric sector, as this influence had significant political ramifications. By the turn of the century, foreign firms were investing gobs of money in technology, education and the exploitation of Norwegian natural resources. German, French and Swiss turbine firms (for example, *Voith, Escher Wyss*, and *Piccard Pictet*) helped to establish the Norwegian production of water turbines, while Swedish, German and Swiss electrical producers (for example, *ASEA, Brown Bovery, AEG, Siemens*, and *NEBB*) bought up local firms and/or established local subsidiaries that exploited their patents and know-how in the electric sector. By 1906, three quarters of all hydroelectric installations yielding more than 3,000 HP were already owned by foreigners (Derry 1973: 197).

Similarly, foreign money was instrumental to the development of Norway's synthetic fertilizer industry, as described in previous chapters. *Norsk Hydro* was originally financed with the help of the Wallenberg brothers and their *Stockholm Enskilda Bank* (in Sweden). Knut Wallenberg was then instrumental in getting the French *Banque de Paris et des Pays-Bas* involved in the project. Later, in 1906-11, *Hydro* cooperated with the German chemical giant, *Badische Anilin und Sodafabrikk* (*BASF*), which was subsequently replaced by a French and Canadian group in 1911 (Hodne and Grytten 1992: 42).

In short, the influence of foreign capital in Norwegian industry was shockingly large, especially when one considers that this influence was being wielded at a time of growing national awareness. In 1891 there were only 350 foreign holding companies in Norway, but by 1910 this number had skyrocketed to 1600. Worse, the nature of Norwegian equity law allowed this foreign capital to circulate anonymously, making it difficult for the authorities to know who actually owned what and when. To Norwegian voters it seemed increasingly as though big Swedish investors (such as Nils Persson and Marcus Wallenberg) owned Norway's crown jewels: its natural resources. By 1905, these voters came to wonder if Sweden still controlled Norway's purse strings, even after formal political independence.

In the first decade of the new century, when nationalist sentiments were on the rise, this imposing role played by foreign capital interests became a major political issue. The ridiculously cheap sale of the falls at Rjukan (see Chapter 3) led to a public outcry that resulted in the Michelsen government's 'Panic Law' in April 1906. This law imposed a temporary ban on the purchase of waterfalls by foreign citizens or by limited companies which might conceal foreign interests. In June (two months later), the prohibition was extended with a second temporary law that covered forest and mining properties and required that any company receiving a concession must have its seat of management in Norway. By 1907, the hiring-out of hydroelectric power was also put under public control (Derry 1973: 198). All companies—regardless of their form—had to get state permission to exploit any of these natural resources. The law included a number of explicit conditions on the buying and selling of these resources, and political authorities were given great power to influence these decisions. The most important of these was that property ownership of a waterfall (and the installations to exploit it) was only granted for a limited time, and the ownership rights would revert to the state after 60 to 80 years. (For ownership in mines, the reversion period was 40 to 80 years.) Thus, private ownership of natural resources was not indefinite, but limited in time.

The most important law for industrial and trade establishments was passed on 14 December 1917, and amended in 1925. The 1917 law imposed a number of mandatory conditions on foreign ownership, including the following: the corporation's seat had to be located in Norway; a majority of the board of directors had to be Norwegian citizens; a certain part of the capital stock had to be in Norwegian hands; Norwegian capital was to be given equal opportunity to share in any extension of a corporation's share capital; employers (in isolated areas) were to be granted fringe benefits including adequate housing, commissary facilities and schools; a certain production fee was to be paid to the Norwegian government; the property could not be sold or transferred without permission; and preference would be given to Norwegian labor and materials (Stonehill 1965: 29).

In short, foreign direct investment in Norway was increasingly placed under the regulatory watch of government officials. This regulation soothed nationalist concerns in the population at a time of increasing political awareness and in the wake of Norway's political independence from Sweden. More importantly, this regulation helped to protect and nourish infant Norwegian industries in several developing branches. One can only speculate about whether Norwegian industrialization would have taken root and expanded without the initial protection provided by these concession laws.

Conclusion

This chapter has described the state of Norway's capital supply in the four decades prior to World War I. This description aimed to provide a glimpse of the significance that capital markets play in the process of development, and how many developing countries (including Norway at this time) suffer from insufficient domestic capital stocks.

For this reason, I began the empirical discussion with a survey of Norway's domestic capital markets. While this survey allows us to conclude that the domestic capital stock in Norway was surely too small to finance its growing needs, I have tried to emphasize the fact that the domestic markets were developing over time, and remained important sources of finance for most of Norway's economic needs during this period.

But Norway relied heavily on foreign capital to finance its growing industrial needs. This foreign capital was attracted to the largest, most capital intensive, most productive and most export-oriented industries in Norway. With foreign capital filling this important need, however, Norway's domestic capital supply was left to satisfy more traditional and general economic needs. In short, Norway seemed to have struck a happy balance between the capacity of its growing domestic capital market and the demands of an export niche that was expanding rapidly.

While an economic balance may have been reached, it was more difficult to reach a political balance between the demands of foreign financiers and the needs of a young nation. The balance that was eventually struck relied heavily on licensing requirements that helped infant Norwegian industries get established. Foreign technology, skill and capital were absolutely necessary for developing Norway's industrial and export potential. The concession laws helped to ensure that this foreign influence did not simply exploit or flood local conditions—but actually facilitated its growth.

This balanced reliance on international finance is an important piece of a complex puzzle that was Norwegian economic catch-up. The next chapter will describe another important piece of that puzzle: the role of emigration.

Chapter 7

On the Move

'Farewell old mother Norway. I'm leaving now from thee...You are too stingy with our workers, but give a plenty to your learned sons.' —emigrant song[1]

Norwegians were on the move in the closing decades of the 19th century. Migration (both inward and outward) contributed to a remarkable period of industrialization and rapid structural changes in the Norwegian economy, as new hope and livelihoods beckoned the disenchanted across county, country and globe. In this chapter I introduce and examine the complex and varied relationships that link migration and Norway's rapid economic growth prior to World War I.

The scale of Norwegian emigration to the Americas was phenomenally large: only the Irish sent a greater share of their population abroad during this period. Indeed, in the most active decade of Norwegian emigration, from 1880 to 1890, about ten per cent of the country's population emigrated. The extent of this Norwegian exodus was bound to have significant economic and political consequences.

But mapping the nature of these consequences is not entirely straightforward. For most contemporary economists, international migration is not a usual or common factor to consider when explaining economic development. Remarkably, some of the most influential textbook accounts of the European industrial revolution and economic development delegate little or no role to migration.[2]

For this reason, it behooves us to spend some time considering how migration relates to economic development. We can then turn to a description of the role played by emigration in the Norwegian context.

---

[1] From Semmingsen (1980: 112).

[2] For an example of the former, see Heilbroner (1985); for an example of the latter, see Paul A. Samuelson (1976). An important exception is the work of Arthur Lewis (see text), which was tested with great success in Kindleberger (1967).

Migration and economic growth

For classical economists, immigration and demographic factors played a central role in explaining economic growth. For example, the eminent Swedish economist Knut Wiksell (1882) openly advocated outward migration from Sweden in order to help the local (poor) peasantry. Indeed, this relationship was not lost on Harry Johnson who—as recently as 1967—noted that the immigration policies of the developed world lay at the core of the development problem (1967: 107). For a number of reasons, however, immigration seldom plays an influential role in contemporary discussions about development.

Remarkably—and in contrast to a vast literature on the effects of international investment and trade on development—the economic literature on international migration and development is relatively small. One important reason for this lacuna is the immensely complicated ways in which migration affects development in both host and sending countries.[3] Another reason may lie in the fact that international migration has been relatively limited at the close of the 20th century. Hence, most contemporary economists tend to believe that restricted labor mobility is a 'natural' state of affairs.

A third and related reason for this silence may be that the effects of migration can be easily subsumed under contemporary trade theory, as described in Chapter 5. Standard trade models, resting on the work of Heckscher, Ohlin and Samuelson (H-O-S), begin by assuming that labor is immobile across countries, and hold that labor-abundant countries will export those goods that require intensive labor inputs to production. In a sense, these countries are seen to export labor: the trading of goods substitutes for the trading of people.

International migration is easy to understand within an H-O-S framework: it occurs in response to differences in wage rates, and continues until some sort of (international) wage-rate equilibrium is achieved. H-O-S approaches assume that countries would like to trade factor services but are unable to do so; instead of factor services they trade goods, as traded goods and services indirectly exploit the factor services embodied in them. Thus, a nation with an abundance of capital and a scarcity of labor is expected to export capital services and import labor ones. Subsequently, it is quite common for economists to view international trade and international migration as similar phenomena, both of which can be analyzed using an H-O-S approach to factor-price equalization.

As a consequence, neo-Ricardian trade theory has often functioned as an excuse for rich countries to erect, protect, and legitimate substantial barriers to immigration from the developing world. International trade is seen as a tide that can lift all boats (both rich and poor) on the basis of comparative advantage. Because of this, international migration is unnecessary: it is argued that trade alone can reduce the rich-poor wage differentials that are often assumed to drive international migration.

---

[3] For a thorough review of this literature along these lines, see Skeldon (1997).

While this represents the most common understanding of the relationship between migration and trade, several economists have shown that by changing some of the underlying assumptions in the H-O-S framework,[4] migration can actually complement (rather than substitute for) trade.   Under these alternative conditions, trade alone does not bring about factor-price equalization, and factor movements (for example, labor migration) between two economies can actually lead to an increase in the volume of commodity trade.   Thus, it is quite possible that international migration actually boosts world trade, rather than substitutes for it.

For development economists, migration has played a much more significant role—but the focus has been on internal, not international, migration. Most of the reason for this can be traced to the work of the Nobel laureate, Arthur Lewis.   Lewis (1954) was interested in estimating how high industrial wages needed to be in order to attract labor from the traditional to the industrial sector.[5] This approach can also be used to emphasize how migration can be seen as a process by which surplus labor in the traditional (rural) sector is released to provide the workforce for the modern (urban) industrial economy.

The particular mechanism of this (development) linkage is the relative wage in the rural and urban sectors.   As workers are encouraged to migrate from wage-poor agricultural jobs to better-paying urban jobs, employers in the agricultural sector find it necessary to increase their wages and/or adopt more productive techniques.   On the other hand, cheap (and deep) pools of labor facilitate the industrial transformation in urban centers.   Both transformations are essential components of development.

Obviously, a similar mechanism is in effect when workers are attracted to better-paying jobs overseas.   As international migration decreases the overall pool of workers in a country, it increases the wages and the bargaining power of the workers that remain.[6]   While significant levels of urban emigration may deplete the urban labor-surplus, much international migration was (at least originally) from rural areas.   In this way, emigration to the New World served as an important buffer against the periodic upswings and downswings in the course of European economic development.

---

[4] Two of these changed assumptions include recognizing the potential costs of migration and constraints on capital. See Markusen (1983) for an example.

[5] Lewis emphasized that the traditional sector is not limited to rural or agricultural production—it can also include urban activities such as petty retail trade, handicrafts and domestic services.

[6] Another way to conceptualize this is to consider how emigration reduces the amount of surplus labor. As 'surplus labor' refers to workers that are not really needed (but who participate in production as a mechanism for income distribution), the workers that remain after emigration will be able to produce as much as before (when there were more workers) but they would not have to share the income with so many others. In this way, sending country incomes can increase as a result of international emigration. I am grateful to Maggi Brigham for pointing this out to me.

Not surprisingly, economic historians have shown the strongest interest in the impact of international immigration on development. For them, there is little doubt that the European economies benefited greatly from open migration to the New World at the turn of the previous century. The Norwegian experience is just one of several that illustrate how some of the fastest economic growth performances in the late 19th century were major ports of emigration to the New World.

For example, in their impressive study of the *Age of Mass Migration*, Hatton and Williamson (1998: 225ff) suggest that mass migration accounted for 208 (!) per cent of the real wage convergence observed between the New and Old Worlds between 1870 and 1910.[7] Although much of this convergence depended on corollary factors (for example, capital accumulation forces, trade and technological catch-up), a significant proportion can be attributed to the mass migrations. Indeed, as we have seen in earlier chapters, all of these factors were at play in the Norwegian case.

Generally, migration can influence international development in four inter-related ways. First, international migration allows for a more efficient matching of international supplies and demand for labor. This has the potential to generate enormous efficiency gains internationally, as shown by Hatton and Williamson's work, described above, as well as a number of more recent and theoretical approaches.[8] Second, emigration tightens the sending-country labor markets, strengthening the bargaining position of the labor that remains (although this strengthening may occur at the expense of international price competitiveness). Third, migrant labor provides a large and dependable source of development capital in the form of remittances. Finally, returning migrants bring capital, skills and market access that benefit the sending economy.

This last influence might be understood in terms of endogenous growth theory, where the Old World's growth is explained by its changing level of human (not natural or institutional) capital. To the extent that emigration favored young adults, and to the extent that a significant percentage of these returned home after obtaining new skills and capital in America, then the impact of migration on the level of human capital in the home (sending) country was potentially tremendous.

Finally, I might briefly mention the issue of 'brain drain', as this is often used to counter any discussion of the potential development effects of migration. Many of today's poorest countries have problems retaining a skilled workforce, as their most promising and elite workers are attracted to jobs in the developed world.

---

[7] This convergence share is so large because some of the convergence effects (in particular, the effects of capital mobility) work in the opposite direction in the aggregate Atlantic economy. See Hatton and Williamson (1998: 225ff) for further elaboration.

[8] Using computable general equilibrium models, this work has suggested that the efficiency gains from freer migration could absolutely dwarf the gains from other, more traditional, development approaches. See, for example, Winters (2002); Iregui (2005) and Moses and Letnes (2004, 2005).

Thus, emigration is often described as a deterrent to economic growth in the developing world.[9] In the late 19th century, however, emigration was not usually an elite endeavor: most migrants were young and without skills. As a result, there was little concern about brain drain in the home (sending) countries. To the contrary, political and economic elites in the sending countries usually advocated emigration, as evidenced by the reference to Wicksell at the start of this section.

In conclusion, we can expect emigration to have affected Norwegian economic development in three (related) ways. First, like internal migration from rural to urban centers, international migration led to a convergence of wages between traditional and modern sectors of the economy (and, of course, between sending and receiving countries). The resulting rise in rural wages forced farmers to pay better wages (which, in turn, encouraged multiplier effects) and/or to adopt new (more productive) technologies. Second, these new conditions strengthened the relative bargaining power of labor vis-à-vis capital. This new bargaining power was partly the result of labor's increased (relative) scarcity, and partly a result of its threat to exit. Finally, emigrants introduced new capital and skills to the Norwegian economy. Like migrant workers today, 19th century immigrants sent a significant proportion of their wages home in the form of remittances— providing a new source of capital for small farmers and entrepreneurs in the home country. In addition, returning émigrés brought home skills, norms, and capital that rejuvenated the Norwegian economy.

The scope of Norwegian emigration

Starting in the mid 1820s, the first waves of Atlantic emigration from Norway were mostly driven by political, social and religious motives. While economic concerns did not seem to play an important role in motivating the first émigrés, they became increasingly important in the latter half of the century. As the economic conditions in Norway worsened in the 1850s and 1860s, emigration was encouraged by a number of political movements (including, most notably, the Thrane movement: see Chapter 3) and by news from America on the bounty awaiting future immigrants. Apparently, this sort of encouragement was so convincing that poor commissions in some Norwegian communities helped to buy tickets for families who wished to immigrate to America.[10]

As illustrated in Figure 7.1, Norwegian emigration during this period can be categorized in terms of three waves peaking in 1869, 1882 and 1903. At its peak (in 1882), fifteen Norwegians out of every thousand were leaving the country

---

[9] There is a growing revisionist literature that challenges this depiction. See Faini (2005) for a brief introduction.

[10] Hovde (1934: 272) reports of rumors where Norwegian poor-relief boards provided prospective paupers with the funds for emigration. Apparently it was cheaper to send them to America than maintain them at home for the rest of their lives.

in hopes of a better life abroad. Nearly 29,000 people left Norway that year. Over the entire period of this study (1865-1914) almost 680,000 people left a country whose 1914 population numbered under 2.5 million residents.

These waves of exodus siphoned off a significant proportion of Norway's birth surplus (in other words, the difference between total born and total dead in a given period). Thus, in the first wave (from 1866-1873), 111,000 people immigrated to the USA—representing some 59 per cent of the birth surplus. During the second wave, from 1879-1893, it is estimated that 250,000 people immigrated to the USA (60 per cent of Norway's birth surplus); and the third wave (1900-1910) washed another 200,000 Norwegians onto American shores (again, 60 per cent of Norway's birth surplus).[11] Over the entire period—stretching from the end of the American Civil War until the start of World War I—well over 40 per cent of Norway's natural demographic increase was lost to emigration (Moe 1970: 267).

Another way to estimate the magnitude of this migration is to consider a simple counterfactual scenario, in which we compare Norway's demographic trajectory against estimates of what that trajectory would look like in the absence of emigration. This juxtapositioning needs to be done dynamically, in order to capture changing demographic conditions (even though the Norwegian fertility rate did not change until after 1900). The difference between these two trajectories can then be attributed to emigration.

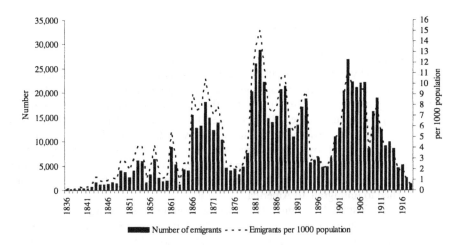

Figure 7.1   Norwegian emigration

Source: SSB (1965: 158)

---

[11] The emigration and birth surplus figures are from Hodne and Grytten (2000: 130).

In this way, Hodne and Grytten (2000: 130) suggested that if Norway maintained its demographic growth rate from the period 1845-1865 (1.3 per cent) and projected it into the near future, then its 1895 population would have been 2.5 million (and in 1920: 3.4 million). However, Norway's actual population in those two years was 2.1 and 2.6 million. In short, the gap between the counterfactual and the actual population in 1920 was 800,000 people (or almost 31 per cent of the actual 1920 population)!

More difficult to measure is the rate of return for Norwegian emigrants. There are no proper statistical data on immigration to Norway during this period. Still, the Norwegian Statistical Bureau (SSB 1965: 218) has used demographic trends to estimate that about one in four (25 per cent) Norwegian émigrés to the New World eventually returned. These returning émigrés would come to play a significant role in Norway's economic catch-up.

The economic effect of Norwegian emigration

Given that emigrants tended to be young, male, and able-bodied, this sort of demographic hemorrhage was bound to have a significant effect on the labor force that remained in Norway.

Of course, the rate of emigration varied significantly from region to region across Norway. As was hinted at in Chapter 4, a drastic decline in the traditional shipping industry in the 1880s and 1890s encouraged much outward migration. Indeed, these migrants make up a significant part of the second emigration wave in Figure 7.1, as that wave corresponds with the decline in the traditional shipping industry which dominated southern Norway. As a result of these economic difficulties, the country's biggest shipping regions in Southern Norway experienced the highest rates of emigration.

Overall, the rural labor force was surely hit hardest, as—until the 1870s— most emigration was from Norway's rural districts, as evidenced in Figure 7.2 below (although large numbers also moved annually to the urban centers to compete for employment).

A series of counterfactual analyses done by Kevin O'Rourke and Jeffrey Williamson (2000: 155) have provided some concrete estimates of the effect of this emigration on the Norwegian labor supply and its wage rate. In particular, we learn that Norway's adjusted net migration rate over the 1870-1910 period was - 5.25 (per thousand per annum), or 19 per cent of the population. In terms of the labor force, the effect was -6.93 (per thousand per annum), or -24 per cent. The impact of this migration can be summarized by the following statistics: because of emigration, Norwegian real wages were 9.7 per cent higher (actual vs. counterfactual); the GDP/capita level was 3.1 per cent higher; and the GDP/worker level was 10.4 per cent higher (again, over the same period, 1870-1914) than would have been the case without emigration. In short, the direct effect of emigration was a significant boost to the national economy.

By bleeding off surplus labor, wages accelerated across the country. If O'Rourke and Williamson's estimates are accurate, we can expect that a nearly ten per cent increase in real wages would have significant political and economic consequences.   Indeed, the Norwegian emigrant commission [*Utvandrings-komiteen*] of 1912-13 seemed to have concurred, arguing that emigration had been instrumental in promoting the mechanization and rationalization of industrial production by contributing to the rise in wages (p. 216).

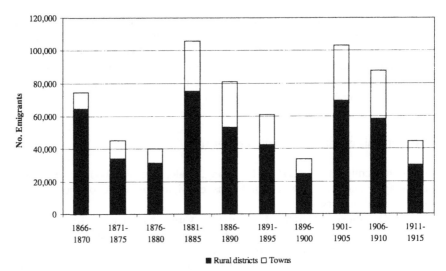

Figure 7.2   Emigration from rural and urban Norway

Source: SSB (1965: 164)

This sort of general wage influence would bring significant political and economic consequences (as described in more detail below), but emigration also made a tremendous impact on a number of specific sectors of the Norwegian economy. To illustrate this impact, we might consider the effect of emigration on two important, if very different, sectors in the Norwegian economy at the time: the traditional agricultural sector and the growing shipping industry.

The effect of emigration on Norwegian farming can be traced through a number of direct and indirect channels. The most important of these concerns the farmer's shrinking profit margin. Norwegian peasants, in the late 19th century, faced a number of threatening challenges. As already described in Chapters 4 and 8, boatloads of cheap imported food were forcing many farmers off the land. At the same time, industrial developments were radically changing the nature and scale of agricultural production—and this was encouraging a new rationalization of land-holdings.

These conditions were not unique to Norway—most European farmers found themselves facing similar pressures. As Kindleberger (1951: 37) explains, European states relied on different policy responses for dealing with the period's increased agricultural competition:

In Britain agriculture was permitted to be liquidated.   In Germany large-scale agriculture sought and obtained protection for itself.   In France, where the demography patterns of resources, and small scale of industrial enterprise favored farming, agricultural as a whole successfully defended its position with tariffs.   In Italy the response was to emigrate.   In Denmark, grain production was converted to animal husbandry.

The Norwegian response relied on a combination of these strategies. Like farmers in Germany (though less effectively), Norwegian farmers began to organize and press for greater tariff protection.   Like their Danish brethren, Norwegian farmers were forced to adapt to new agricultural techniques and market niches to avoid direct competition with cheaper American grains.   But the Norwegian response was most like the Italian: emigration was used to release pent-up pressures on agriculture.

While emigration can be understood as a response to increased international competition in agricultural products, it also had its own, independent, effects on the development of Norwegian agriculture.   In particular, massive emigration encouraged Norwegian farmers to adopt less labor-intensive production practices—they needed to invest in machinery and techniques that increased productivity without extra manpower.   Only in this way could Norwegian farmers manage with a shrinking supply of local labor, and/or avoid paying it higher wages.

Emigration also reduced the potential pool of independent farmers, so that the price of agricultural land did not rise as quickly as the general price level. This created new opportunities for smallholders/crofters to purchase land, and for family plots to be rationalized in a more productive way. At any rate, this was the conclusion of an 1845 ministerial committee that was assembled to report on the problem of emigration: emigration had helped to retard the process of excessive parcellization by getting rid of potential 'heirs'.[12]

Finally, emigrant remittances were an important source of new capital, skills and norms for Norwegian farmers. Returning émigrés brought with them money, experience and techniques that were quickly employed in the Norwegian context.   Indeed, the above-mentioned *Utvandringskomiteen* estimated that the annual sum of (fiscal) remittances then amounted to about $10,000,000 (p. 217). This was not a trivial amount, but approximately what Norway was spending on sickness insurance in 1927 or 1928 (Hovde 1934: 260). Consequently, emigration was both a useful (and necessary) adjustment mechanism to an increasingly global marketplace—it facilitated a more streamlined, modern and productive agricultural sector in Norway.

This was clearly evident in the 1912-13 *Utvandringskomiteen*'s report on the effect of emigration:

---

[12] *Stortingsforhandlinger, 1845, Propositioner, No. 6*, p. 27.

> The returned Americans put their stamp upon it all; the rural districts are hardly recognizable. Farmers are not so burdened with debt as before; people live better, eat better, clothe themselves better; —thus the population itself improves. All those who come from America begin to till the soil better than it was tilled before...Crop rotation is introduced, machinery is acquired, the building of the farm, dwellings as well as others, are improved, more rational dairy methods are practiced, and gardens are laid out. In all these respects there have been great advances in *Sörlandet* [the southern region of the country] during the past 10-15 years; the returned Americans have had their very considerable part in it, in some places even the largest part. They bring home with them much practical experience and understanding, which works to the advantage of the whole region. Furthermore, they have a will to take hold, and have in America learned a rate of work, which is different from what people are accustomed to here at home (p. 3).[13]

While Norwegian agriculture was forced to adapt to the threat of increased trade and the cost of emigration, the effects of these same developments were more welcomed in the Norwegian shipping industry. Indeed, the Norwegian shipping industry received considerable early stimulus from emigrant traffic. Already in the late 1830s, when Norwegian emigration began in earnest, some Norwegian vessels began to specialize in the traffic. The 1845 ministerial commission on emigration recognized as much—it refused to impose stricter emigration restrictions for fear of the effect this would have on the Norwegian export and shipping industries:

> This freightage of human beings probably has provided the opportunity to exploit more profitably the American market for the products of the Norwegian iron foundries, so that this industry, which is so important for our country, and which gives employment to a not inconsiderable number of citizens, of late has taken on new life, after having been threatened with collapse as the result of the prevailing unfortunate trade conditions...[14]

This fortuitous mix of Norwegian trade, shipping and emigration is clearly evident after Great Britain repealed its Navigation Laws in 1849. Suddenly, Norwegian ships had access to the lucrative intra-commonwealth trade, and emigrants were useful cargo for (otherwise empty) Norwegian ships plying the Atlantic. While the end destination for most Norwegian emigrants continued to be the United States, they were increasingly channeled through the port of Quebec. In this way, Norwegian ships could carry emigrants and freight to Quebec and return to a British port with Canadian lumber in the hold. Later on, after the turn of the century, return visits by émigrés and tourists made it increasingly possible for passenger vessels to fill berths on the homeward voyage as well.

---

[13] Translation from Hovde (1934: 278).

[14] *Stortingsforhandlinger, 1845, Propositioner, No.6*, pp. 26-27, translated by Hovde (1934: 261-2).

By the mid 19th century this industry was growing rapidly. In 1848, about 1,400 Norwegians crossed the Atlantic; in the following year the number rose to 4,000 passengers, requiring 24 vessels to carry the direct passenger traffic to New York. By 1854, nearly fifty Norwegian emigrant vessels had landed at Quebec (Blegen 1931: 267, 356). With a market that was expanding so rapidly (and lucratively), most of the best Norwegian sailing vessels were engaged in emigrant traffic at mid century.

After 1850, however, foreign countries began to capture and dominate the world shipping industry, employing better and faster ships than Norway. Because Norway was relatively tardy in the transition to iron and steam, the demands of emigrant traffic (for speed and comfort) provided an important impetus for reviving (and modernizing) the Norwegian ship-building industry.

A popular anecdote on the rebirth of the Norwegian shipping industry illustrates the potential spill-over effects of emigration on economic development. Norwegian 19th century history is filled with stories of young adventurers who travel to America in search of a fortune. Among them were Jens Gram and Annanias Dekke, who went to the US to study clipper ships in the mid 1800s with an eye at exploiting this type of ship's potential in the lucrative passenger (trans-Atlantic migrant) market. Upon learning its secrets, Gram and Dekke returned to Bergen in the mid 1850s to build ships modeled after John Griffith's 'China clippers'. The success of their import is almost legendary in Norway, as these China clipper copies came to dot the whole coast of Norway.

The experience of Gram and Dekke was duplicated in countless sectors of the Norwegian economy: return emigration brought with them capital, skills and markets that were critical sparks for igniting Norwegian economic development. Small entrepreneurs popped up everywhere, copying foreign designs and products, and (as a consequence) developing new domestic markets.

Equally important was the fact that home-bound émigrés returned with a different perspective on the world and their experiences of the outside world proved to be a powerful force for change. Along with money, skills and habits, returning émigrés arrived with new ideas about the poverty and powerlessness from which they fled.

The political effect of emigration

Few political entities can sit idly as a significant share of their population defects to greener pastures. Norway, at the turn of the 20th century, was no exception. As the number of potential emigrants rose, they began to pose a significant economic and political challenge to the Norwegian authorities. Desperately, the authorities began to search for a way to discourage massive emigration.

Among others, Hovde (1934: 257) suggests that mounting emigration was a primary incentive for increased government involvement in Norwegian economic life at the time, as described in Chapters 3 (above) and 8 (below). New economic opportunities (in the form of extending the railroad, highway and telegraph networks, for example) were seen as important and necessary measures to mop-up the potential demand for emigration. Indeed, as early as 1842, the editor of the *Christiansandsposten* newspaper urged the state to promote the settlement of uncultivated land at home as a way to deter emigration (Blegen 1931: 157-8).

The Norwegian government's interpretation was very similar. Indeed, the first formal national response to the threat of emigration came already in 1845, when a ministerial committee was assembled to report on the problem of emigration.[15] Later, in 1912-13, another commission [*Utvandringskomiteen*] expressed the conviction that the causes of emigration were fundamentally economic, and that the only effective deterrent to emigration was the promotion of domestic industry and agriculture by public and private agencies (p. 217).

Concomitantly, a number of anti-emigration societies were beginning to form at the turn of the century—groups such as New Soil [*Ny Jord*] and the League of Norwegians [*Normandsforbundet*] developed a series of programs aimed at removing the economic basis for emigration. For example, *Ny Jord* raised funds— partly by subscription, and partly by state appropriations—to develop a new land policy that could stave off emigration.

The very scale of Norwegian emigration forced the authorities to examine Norway's economic and social structure, and to undertake a critical study of her social institutions. Social maladies were recognized as important factors that stimulated emigration, and activists often used the threat of emigration to pressure for reforms. Indeed, the 1845 report suggested that pressure from emigration deserves much of the credit for the level of religious freedom found in the Scandinavian countries.[16]

Nowhere, perhaps, was this pressure more evident than in the nascent Norwegian labor movement. While emigration provided a safety valve for social discontent, it also created the necessary conditions for a vigorous labor movement. Although it is feasible that these two effects can lead in different directions, there is evidence to suggest that they complemented one another in the Norwegian context.

On the one hand, the American frontier worked for Norway like it did for the US: as a haven of refuge for the unemployed and socially discontented. Indeed, Norway's unfortunate class of cotters [*husmænd*], which constituted one of the chief elements in Norway's social ferment at mid century, disappeared partly because of emigration. Similarly, working-class groups often resorted to emigration as an avenue of escape.

On the other hand, as noted by the *Utvandringskomiteen* (p. 216), emigration created the prerequisites for social reform and progressive struggle, and encouraged the Left to press its demands. The lives of two of Norway's leading

---

[15] While the Swedish Academy of Science had (already in 1763) offered a prize for a study of the causes and cure (of the then miniscule level) of emigration, this Norwegian report was the earliest of its kind in Scandinavia. The report can be found in *Stortingsforhandlinger, 1845, Propositioner, No. 6.*

[16] *Stortingsforhandlinger, 1845, Propostioner, No. 6,* p. 25.

activists from this period illustrate the impact of emigration on the Norwegian labor movement. At the height of his political career, Marcus Thrane openly advocated organized emigration as an instrument for forcing Norwegian elites to recognize the value of labor; he himself moved to the United States (and died there) after being released from a Norwegian prison in 1858. Later, Martin Tranmael also benefited significantly from his immigrant experience in America. Much of Tranmael's tactical education and experience can be attributed to his exposure with the radical International Workers of the World (IWW) movement while himself an immigrant to the US Pacific Coast.

Conclusion

While it is difficult to provide any reliable figure about the economic and political effects of emigration on Norwegian economic development, the two are clearly related. Sophisticated counter-factual and computable general equilibrium analyses have demonstrated that emigration played a significant role in explaining Norway's remarkable economic catch-up to the period's wealthiest states. These analyses find a clear connection between rising real wages and GDP (in both per worker, and per capita terms) on the one hand, and emigration to the New World on the other.

In addition, American immigrants sent a substantial amount of money home in the form of remittances. Semmingsen (1980: 164) claims that remittances totaling some 20 million kroner were sent back to Norway in 1905. This is sizeable amount of money: the total value of Norwegian imports from the US at the time was just 15-18 million kroner, and Norway's national budget totaled just 90-100 million kroner!

While emigration played an important role in raising domestic wages in Norway, its effect on the domestic norms, skills, and even capital levels (by way of the returning émigré) should not be underestimated. All in all, emigration played an important part in encouraging the industrial transformation and economic growth that characterized this period of Norwegian history.

At the same time, emigration functioned as a useful release valve for the pent-up pressures associated with the liberalization of world grain markets and the transformation of the Norwegian economy to a more industrial footing. The threat of mass exit sharpened the attention of political authorities, and encouraged them to think in ways that could discourage migration. Social, political and economic reforms were a very important part of this enticement campaign. These developments, in turn, had a significant—if indirect—effect on subsequent economic development.

In short, the Atlantic economy prior to World War I offered hundreds of thousands of poor and desolate Norwegians the opportunity for a better life in the New World. For the Norwegians that remained, massive emigration helped to reduce demographic pressures, to improve the bargaining position of the disadvantaged, and to stimulate a more vibrant economic environment with new skills, norms, markets and capital.

What is most remarkable about Norway's Cinderella story is not that so many people left for new adventures and fairy-tale lives in the New World, or that this mass emigration contributed to a more vibrant domestic economy for the Norwegians that stayed. What is most remarkable, perhaps, is that any state today can manage a similar economic transformation without access to massive emigration.

Chapter 8

The End of an Era

In the forty years prior to World War I, several European countries experienced an economic roller-coaster ride that ended with industrialization and economic modernization. Over the period 1870 to 1913, Europe's aggregate industrial production index actually increased three-fold: from 51 to 157 (Berend and Ranki 1982: 143). In many important respects, neighboring Sweden and Denmark out-performed Norway over this period. Indeed, several European and New World states clearly benefited from the growing international markets for goods, capital and labor that existed at the turn of the twentieth century. Seen in this light, the Norwegian experience does not appear very unique.

The Norwegian story begins from a position of relatively poverty and proceeds at a rapid pace as she engages international markets to ratchet her wages closer to those in the most advanced economies. From her humble beginnings as an agrarian and fishing-based economy, Norway blossomed into an export-driven producer that could push off of a growing industrial footing. Economic growth, in turn, brought greater demands on a state that was increasingly democratic in nature. Like Cinderella, the Norwegian economy benefited from a benevolent fairy godmother (read hydroelectric power), but she also enjoyed a number of inherently attractive traits (such as access to abundant natural resources), with which a little magic could go a long way.

Norway used the time before World War I to engage international markets and to build up her experience, expertise, and self-confidence— characteristics that were essential for Norway's subsequent development. But Norway's engagement with these markets was radically different than what we would see after World War II, when Norway's economic record is all the more remarkable. Indeed, Norway's relationship to these markets changed over the period under consideration. In the early years, the state's involvement was mostly limited to setting the larger parameters for encouraging economic growth and development. Over time, the state would become increasingly interventionist and protective of nascent democratic interests.

As late 19th century economic growth began to take hold, and as the shortcomings of liberalism and unfettered markets became increasingly obvious, the Norwegian state began to branch off into new areas of activity. Thus, at the turn of the century we begin to see the state acting more and more as an arbitrator between different interest groups and their relationship to liberal markets (for example, between economic concerns in the exposed versus sheltered sectors, or between the organized interests of labor and capital). While the state's scope of activity at this time was always limited by its ability to secure adequate revenues, it is these sorts of state activities that become even more important in the interwar and postwar periods.

Indeed, as the interwar economic crises undermined faith in both international markets and the liberal ideology that supported them, the state and indigenous interest organizations began to experiment with new means of economic organization. These experiments drew from a variety of new developments, including a burgeoning cooperative movement, a centralized and hierarchical framework of corporatist institutions representing the interests of capital and labor, a strong and vibrant Labor Party, and a growing commitment to use the state's resources to encourage structural adjustments in the face of changes in the international economy.

We can see the basic outlines of these developments before the outbreak of World War I. After that war, and before the next, these new types of organizations and economic activities begin to take root and grow in a hectic and crisis-laden international economic climate. After World War II, international trade and exchange on all fronts was severely constricted. Labor and capital markets, as well as the trade in goods and services, shrunk with the fear of economic (crisis) contagion and in recognition of the need to rebuild war-torn economies. The institutions, organizations, and philosophy of postwar reconstruction were forged in the economic turmoil of the interwar period.

Discussing these changes could warrant a book in itself. Indeed, very much is already written on Scandinavia's (and Norway's) interwar economic and political transformations. As a consequence, I will only dwell briefly on this period in a short, epilogue, chapter that follows. In the chapter before us, I aim to summarize the nature of Norway's disparate developments over the previous four decades—developments that together constitute the end of an economic era. With World War I came an abrupt end to Norway's first experience with liberalism.

I begin the chapter by summarizing Norway's economic gains at the outbreak of World War I. As I have endeavored to show in the chapters above, these gains can be attributed largely to Norway's engagement with world goods, capital and labor markets. In arguing this, I do not want to encourage students to ignore important domestic factors. Demographic developments, a changing political and legal landscape, and the role of education (for example) are all important variables for explaining 19th and early 20th century economic growth in Norway. But these developments in themselves would have surely dried up without access to greater demand for domestically-produced goods, and better access to cheaper input and consumer goods in Norway.

In the chapter's second section, I illustrate how Norway's engagement with world goods, capital and labor markets should be understood in terms of complements, not substitutes. Market integration across all three fronts allowed Norway to better exploit more market niches. By accessing and exploiting all of these markets, Norwegians undoubtedly increased the potential effect of world trade on its own development. This argument implies that the liberalization of trade and capital markets alone (as we see in today's context) may be insufficient to bring about the sort of economic growth and convergence that Norway, and much of Europe, experienced prior to World War I.

In the chapter's third section, I briefly summarize Norway's political and institutional developments during this period. It is important to remind ourselves that Norway's engagement with international markets did not happen at the expense of political (democratic) development or the expansion of nascent welfare or social policies. Arguably, it was the pressure that originated from international markets, especially foreign capital and labor markets, that facilitated—even encouraged—the expansion of these democratic institutions. Indeed, the Norwegian experience suggests that nation building, independence, democracy, and a certain degree of economic sovereignty were all possible and useful in the turn of the last century's global marketplace for goods, capital and labor.

By concluding the book in this way, I leave the reader to wonder whether developing states today can enjoy conditions that allow them to combine political development and market engagement. I conclude the chapter with some brief speculation about the current international context and the lessons it offers to today's developing states.

An economic summary

Norway's most important, but perhaps least unique, achievement in this period is that she became an industrialized country. For fairly obvious reasons, economic historians have difficulty agreeing about the exact timing of that industrialization, but we can be fairly confident that it occurred sometime before World War I. As I mentioned in Chapter 4, the most common (albeit rough) indicator for measuring a country's industrial transformation is the percentage of people employed in the primary sector. When less than 50 per cent of the population is employed in this sector (which includes fishing, farming and forestry), the country in question is understood to be industrialized. Norway reached this milestone sometime in the 1890s.

Despite disagreement over timing, it should not be controversial to describe Norway's economic modernization in terms of two subsequent waves. The first important wave brought a modernization of traditional sectors, especially the wood products' industry. New technology, capital, and markets encouraged Norwegians to develop new products and production techniques—both of which had important spillover effects for the surrounding economy. Later, as we saw in Chapter 4, Norwegians exploited their enormous hydroelectric potential to stake out a significant presence in the world electrochemical and electrometallurgical industries. As these hydroelectric installations tended to be located in outlying districts, Norway's subsequent industrialization was rather unique in character. Because of these developments, and an increasingly industrialized fishing industry, the Norwegian worker was more likely to live in a rural factory town rather than in a big city. This development facilitated political cooperation between farmers and workers, which—in turn—led to the important 'crisis compromise' that was a central part of the (later) electoral success of Norwegian social democracy, in the interwar and postwar periods.

In describing this economic modernization, it makes little sense to speak of Norway as an innovator—although we do find important innovations in the whaling and electrochemical industries, for example. Rather, Norwegian modernization seemed to rely on Norway's capacity to imitate or copy important developments from abroad. As a general rule of thumb, it might be said that Norwegian industries began by importing machines, processes, skilled labor and capital. With time, Norwegians came to mimic these (imported) processes, they learned to adapt them to Norwegian conditions, and—eventually—Norwegians developed the skills and capacity to continue their development autonomously.

Neither were Norwegians particularly quick to adopt and/or incorporate these new processes and technologies. The tardy transition of Norway's shipping fleet to vessels built in steel and powered by steam is the best known (and perhaps most costly) example of this—but Norway was also slow to mechanize its fishing fleet and to modernize its agricultural production, generally. After all, the first modern factory industry in Norway was introduced in the 1840s, yet it was not until after the Second World War—one hundred years later—that we can begin to speak about a modern industrial structure in Norway.

Still, substantial progress was being made, and this progress might be measured in terms of Norway's dramatic shift in employment away from the local homestead and primary sector, into urban industrial workplaces. Between 1875 and 1920, Norway's total number of gainfully employed rose by almost 50 per cent (from 736,289 to 1,068,175), although their percentage of the relevant population (over 15 years of age) fell slightly (from 61.7 per cent to 59.4 per cent). While these changes were important, agriculture remained the largest employer (by branch) in the 1920s—employing almost 17 per cent of the active labor force. The industrial share was growing rapidly, however, and in 1920 it constituted 12 per cent (SSB 1994: tables 9.1 and 9.2).

One of the most common indicators of economic success (or failure) in the developed world today is a country's level of unemployment. For this reason, some readers may be wondering why we have not discussed Norwegian unemployment at the time. The reason for this is that early unemployment statistics are woefully inadequate. Like many developing countries today, there were simply not enough resources available to count all of the people who were searching for, but unable to find, work. In addition, much unemployment in these kinds of economies is disguised. While it is possible to obtain data for the percentage of unemployed labor union members for as early as 1903 (three per cent), this is hardly a reliable figure for the percentage of unemployed people, nationwide.

Neither was there any real demand for these sorts of statistics. During most of this period, under the reign of classical liberalism, unemployment and poverty were largely understood to be the consequences of (failed) individual decisions. Responsibility for employment was seen to lie with the individual, not with the state, the employer, or the community. As a result, there was little demand to collect aggregate statistics on unemployment.

Thus far we have been focusing on the commonalities between Norway's industrial experiences with those of comparable states. Indeed, I have tried to emphasize how Denmark and Sweden both enjoyed similar economic transformations (the result of also embracing world markets). If Norway is unique, then, it is in the way in which she embraced global markets across all three fronts (goods, capital and labor). While Denmark may have relied more on foreign trade, and Sweden may have been able to exploit world markets for important innovations in its engineering industries (and/or have benefited from profitable outlets for its excess indigenous capital), Norway had the most precarious relationship to all of these markets.

More than its neighbors, Norwegians were dependent upon the import of food stuffs and industrial inputs. Its small agricultural base (itself a consequence of climate and landscape) and its relative underdevelopment (add political subservience or dependency to an unaccommodating climate and landscape) meant that Norway had to rely on world market demand for many of its nascent industrial products. For the same reasons (political domination and poor natural endowments for agriculture) Norway needed to depend more on international capital to finance its industrial take-off and it was destined to experience greater emigration to the New World. In short, Norway had fewer options than either Sweden or Denmark: it had to embrace global markets or risk a return to the political and economic servitude that characterized most of her modern history.

As I have endeavored to show in the pages above, Norway's embrace of these world markets allowed it to catch up to world-market leaders on a number of important indicators. According to a study by Williamson (1996: appendix table 1), Norwegian real wages increased more than any other country in his sample,[1] covering the period 1870 to 1910/1913. In fact, Williamson shows Norwegian real wages to have increased by a remarkable 250 per cent (from 28 to 98 on an index, where real wages were indexed at 1900 = 100)! The rise in Danish real wages is second in that sample, rising 183 per cent.

As the Williamson study uses indices with national base years, it is not very useful for making comparisons across countries. In another paper, co-authored with Alan Taylor (Taylor and Williamson 1994), the authors use real wage comparisons on an index that is based on the real wage in Great Britain in 1905 (=100). With this index, the Norwegian record is less unique, but still impressive. In Figure 8.1, which is derived from the Taylor and Williamson paper, I have divided their sample of seventeen countries into three groups: Scandinavian, European, and New World states. By estimating the percentage change on each of their indicators over the 1870 to 1910 period, we see how remarkable the Scandinavian record is, compared to other European states. In terms of real wages, GDP/capita and GDP/worker, over the 1870 to 1910 period, the Scandinavian countries easily outperformed other countries in Europe. In Norway, real wages

---

[1] Strangely, this sample did not include Sweden, which may have outperformed Norway. Williamson's (1996) sample includes Australia, Canada, USA, Belgium, Denmark, France, Germany, Italy, the Netherlands, Norway, UK, Spain and Portugal.

increased almost 150 per cent—significantly above all the other (non-Scandinavian) countries in the sample. The Norwegian rise in GDP/capita and GDP/worker were also greater than most of the European countries, outside of Scandinavia.

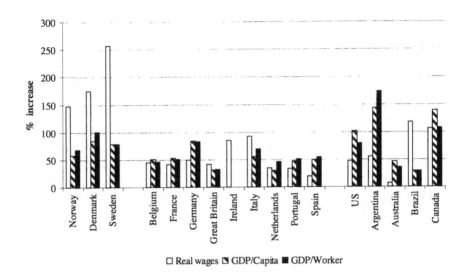

Figure 8.1   International comparisons, 1870-1910*

*Each column represents the percentage increase in real wages, GDP/capita and GDP/worker from 1870 to 1910. See the original source for more information on the nature of the component data in each column.

Source: Taylor and Williamson (1994: table 3)

In short, by exploiting international markets, Norwegian wages were able to rapidly converge on the world's leading wage earners—pushing Norwegian GDP/capita and Norwegian GDP/worker rates higher and higher.

Global connections

For a small country like Norway, engagement with international markets is a basic necessity. In previous chapters, I have simply described the important ways in which Norway has exploited these disparate markets: by importing necessary foodstuffs and industrial inputs; by tapping into world demand for products that can be produced efficiently in Norway; by attracting international skills, technology and capital to develop Norway's industrial potential; and by allowing excess labor to emigrate to places that could better utilize its potential.

In each of the three previous chapters I have shown how different global markets—for goods and services, for capital, and for labor—played an important role in Norwegian development. I have also provided a brief introduction to the sort of economic theories that underlie our understanding of the development effects of trade, investment and migration. In each area there is a substantial theoretical and empirical literature.

In Chapter 5 we learned about how Norway's import of cheap foodstuffs forced an adjustment onto Norwegian agriculture, freeing up much labor that would subsequently find its way into nascent industrial jobs. Freer trade also provided the country with access to essential input goods for Norway's industrial production. More importantly, perhaps, was the fact that world markets could provide enough demand to encourage the exploitation of Norwegian natural resources at a scale that would have been unthinkable given Norway's limited domestic demand.

In Chapter 6 we saw how the Norwegian government and Norwegian industrialists were able to rely on foreign financing to supplement its own, rather limited, domestic supply of capital. This foreign investment was channeled into the largest and most speculative adventures, so that domestic savings could be spread out to meet more traditional investment needs in the home economy. The Norwegian experience is fairly unique in that its history is characterized by periods of significant factor flows to and from other countries. Like Canada and Australia (countries which share the characteristics of a sparse population and large unexploited natural resources), capital imports covered a significant part of Norway's gross domestic investments—more than was common in other developed countries.

Finally, in the last chapter we saw the effect that an exodus of labor could have on domestic labor market conditions. Fewer workers, wielding the threat of exit, were able to secure better wages and better working conditions, in the nascent—but expanding—industrial sector. This, in turn, pressured employers in all sectors to adopt more efficient means of production, in order to avoid rising labor costs. Most importantly, perhaps, was the effect that this threat of exit seemed to have on the political authorities as they tried to accommodate worker demands in fear of an even greater exodus.

But the real gains from embracing late 19th century markets may have been accrued from the complementary effects of tangential global markets. In other words, the existence of contemporaneous markets for goods, capital and labor may have encouraged synergistic effects that improve the effects of trade in each market. If this is true, the overall gains from all three markets might be larger than what we can expect from summing the individual effects of each market.

To give you an idea of how these synergy effects might work, consider the following hypothetical example. A poor, uneducated Norwegian peasant migrates to the US for a twenty-year period, where he learns about new types of produce/products, modern farming techniques, and the power of new producer cooperatives. Returning home, he brings with him that knowledge and skill, along with a sizeable nest-egg which he then invests in his local community: buying a farm and the machinery to run it efficiently. He then works to organize neighboring farmers into a movement that can educate them about more efficient production techniques, about exploiting comparative advantage (so as to not compete with more efficient international producers) and which can allow them to control the market supply of their products. This control could allow the farmers some protection from the radical swings in supply and prices that characterize primary products' markets. From this simple (albeit hypothetical) example, one can begin to see the way in which trade, migration and the import of capital can combine to produce significant multiplier effects in the local economy.

The literature on economic history, referenced above, recognizes the way in which different global-market effects can compound and complement one another. This is clearly documented in work that considers the factors underlying the dramatic convergence of labor productivity rates and real wages among present OECD members before World War I. In this work we find that commodity market, labor market and capital market effects are actually working in different (sometimes opposing) directions! In particular, Taylor and Williamson (1994: 19 and figure 2) estimated that labor market integration forces contributed to 119 per cent of the real wage convergence found in the Atlantic economy, that commodity price conversion contributed 30 per cent toward that convergence, and that a number of residual forces (such as technological catch-up, unmeasured intra-European migration, human capital accumulation, and such) contributed an additional 29 per cent.[2] Remarkably, capital market integration in the Atlantic economy of the time worked in the opposite direction, as it raised wage and labor productivity rates in the rich New World, while lowering wages and labor productivity rates in the poor Old World. The result is an anti-convergence force that Taylor and Williamson estimated to be (-) 79 per cent.

In Norway, of course, the situation was different, and more in-line with traditional economic theory. Unlike the aggregate Atlantic economy, we know that relatively little Norwegian capital fled to the New World. At the time, there was simply very little excess capital to spare. Indeed, as we saw in Chapter 6, Norway found it necessary to attract significant amounts of foreign capital to spark her industrial transformation. Thus, Norway was able to exploit positive convergence effects from all these markets.

Quantitative studies by Riis and Thonstad (1989: 121-2) have used counterfactual computational analyses to segregate and estimate the effects of capital and labor mobility on Norwegian economic development. In the Norwegian case, the outflow of migrants and the inflow of capital tended to work in tandem to increase the country's capital-labor (C/L) ratio, which—in turn—affected the nation's overall economic performance. In particular, Riis and Thonstad find that international emigration and inward international capital flows contributed to a C/L ratio that was eight times larger than it would have been in the absence of these international engagements (over the 1865 to 1915 period). Like Taylor and Williamson (1994), they find that international emigration is clearly the most important factor explaining this boost to Norway's C/L ratio. This boost, in

---

[2] See also Hatton and Williamson (1998) for a more detailed explanation of these effects.

turn, was shown to be responsible for 53 per cent of the growth in Norway's net domestic product per capita (Riis and Thonstad 1989: 126-7).

Democratization and the state

While these economic results are impressive in themselves, they were accompanied by political developments that are often seen as antithetical to globalization today. In particular, the Norwegian government underwent a number of democratic reforms across several fronts. This democratic pressure lead to a substantial change in the government's relationship to the Norwegian economy: it began to regulate, and more actively control, its most sensitive economic sectors.

During the period under study, Norway experienced a radical political transformation. At the beginning of the study, in 1865, Norway was a junior partner in a constitutional monarchy whose sovereign sat on a throne in Stockholm. The role of the government was largely restricted to the sort of night watchman state idealized by liberal philosophy. In the realm of economic exchange, its activities were mostly limited to securing the conditions under which private (and unfettered) markets could function efficiently, to build essential economic infrastructure, and to secure needed funds from foreign markets.

By the outbreak of World War I, Norway enjoyed full independence as a modern parliamentary government built on the principle of universal suffrage. All Norwegian men had won the right to vote in 1898, regardless of property, whereas women did not secure the same right until 1913. Needless to say, this expansion of suffrage—and the (concomitant) rise of new interest group organizations—encouraged the state to become more active in protecting the interests of these new political forces.

Once the constitutional conflict was resolved in 1884, and parliamentarianism was established in the country, the Union with Sweden preoccupied Norwegian politics until they achieved full independence in 1905. While the Union proved popular at first, as it helped to guarantee Norway's security and delivered some economic benefit, Norwegian public opinion grew increasingly critical of its ties to Sweden. Growing nationalism and an increased sense of national self-consciousness in Norway made the ties unbearable, and military preparations on each side began after 1895.

New political parties began to pop up and compete for the votes of an expanding franchise. Some of these new parties, such as the Labor Party (established in 1887), would prove to be extremely influential in the decades that follow. Still, as illustrated in Figure 3.2, the two traditional parties (Venstre and Høyre) continued to dominate the political landscape (although the Labor Party was narrowing the distance) in the first decades of the 20th century.

While the 1880s brought parliamentarianism, the 1890s saw the increased influence of special-interest groups that mirrored the most important cleavages in Norwegian society (for example, gender, language and economic interests). By the end of the century, large organizations representing the interest of capital (NAF) and labor (LO) demanded and won the right to be heard before the Storting on important national policies that would affect their interests. Likewise, important cooperative producer movements were established, and their influence spread dramatically; by 1906 the cooperative movement had established a national organization, *Norges Kooperative Landsforening* (NKL). Nearly all of these organizations got their inspiration and experience from similar movements abroad.

With the extension of the franchise and the influence of these new interest organizations, the Norwegian state had to take better care of its (now voting) population. As a consequence of these democratic pressures, the state's role gradually transformed from that of organizing and encouraging economic growth and development, to regulating and arbitrating between conflicting interests within the economy. Thus, from the 1880s, conflicts over the tariff question became increasingly important, leading to moderate protection in 1897 and 1905. The concession laws of 1909, described in Chapters 3 and 6, were also the direct result of public pressures. In addition, the state began to impose a number of regulations aimed at improving working conditions and protecting employees against injury at the workplace.[3] As a consequence, new limits were placed on the employment of women and children, and industrial machinery was made safer to use. In short: armed with the vote and a threat of exit, the interests of the Norwegian people prevailed, and the state was transformed.

When labor market conflicts (strikes and lock-outs) began to make a serious (negative) impact on the national economy, the state again intervened and took over the role of arbitrator. Indeed, the Liberal Party wanted to outlaw strikes and lock-outs and force parties to settle their differences under compulsory arbitration. While this Liberal (!) vision did not prevail, the system that was established in 1915 distinguished between legal and illegal conflicts. As a result, conflicts over pay and working conditions were first channeled through compulsory mediation before a strike or lock-out could be called.

Although these new state activities proved popular, they were also expensive. Like many countries in Europe at the time, the Norwegian government was desperately searching for new sources of government revenue. After all, the existing tax system was particularly vulnerable to democratization and globalization, as agriculture and tariffs were then the main tax bases for governments. The government's dilemma was clear: the vote made it increasingly difficult to rely on the one, and international agreements made it more difficult to rely on the other. Like other countries, Norway's response was to rely more heavily on a progressive income tax.

---

[3] These pressures were met in 1885, when a unanimous Storting appointed an important Labor Commission. A new labor protection law in 1892 (updated in 1909) forbade the employment of children under twelve in factories, but allowed teenagers (age 14-18) to work a ten hour day, but not at night. With a law in 1894, Norwegian industrial workers were granted accident insurance (a provision that was extended to fishermen in 1908 and seamen in 1911). In 1901, a national insurance institution [*Riksforsikringsanstalten*] was set up, followed by a program for unemployment insurance (1906), and (in 1909) compulsory health insurance for some of the actively employed (Hodne 1981: 427-8).

From today's perspective, the biggest constraint on government spending may have been its commitment to balanced budgets. There was, as yet, little sympathy for the need or utility of counter-cyclical spending patterns.[4] As illustrated in Figure 8.2, Norway followed virtually every country in Europe by trying to balance its budget, year after year. Although the government's revenues and expenditures grew substantially in the years before the war, the state remained mostly committed to balancing its budget each year.

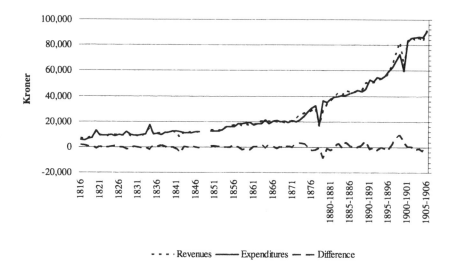

Figure 8.2   Government finances, 1816-1905*

* I am grateful to Camilla Brautaset for providing me with the data in this figure. See the original piece for details about the different sources that make up this time series.

Source: Brautaset (2001: 47)

In short, this period of economic globalization was accompanied by an impressive political transformation which ended with the establishment of new political organizations, a more active and interventionist state, and an increased willingness by political authorities to respect the political power of the new and expanding franchise. At the beginning of the period, Norwegian and international exchange was largely unregulated. Labor markets were flexible, as trade unions were relatively weak. Economic globalization spread without any supranational institutions that could function as lenders of last resort. The early context was, in many respects, a textbook example of classical liberalism.

---

[4] Although a liberal Norwegian economist, Oskar Jæger, was already beginning to contemplate the effects of counter-cyclical budgets in a 1930 publication—so the ideas were floating around.

Over time, however, things changed. People came to recognize and fear the enormous injustices created by an unfettered market.   New interest organizations and cooperatives began to wield their influence in order to secure better terms and conditions of trade. An expanding franchise demanded to be heard, and governments responded by imposing a number of regulatory conditions on the workplace, on ownership, and on the right to strike. It was during this period of 19th century liberalization, and in response to it, that a new, more democratic and interventionist state was born.

Reflections on the 19th century

Perhaps I have been too optimistic and generous. By focusing on the international determinants to Norway's economic growth before World War I, I may have implicitly overstated the potential of world markets for today's developing countries. Even if poor countries were able to embrace world markets as part of their development strategies before World War I, it is possible that the nature of today's world markets makes this embrace more difficult and/or less likely to succeed. In this final section, I would like to review some of these caveats, so that the reader will have difficulty in concluding that the Norwegian economic path is easy to follow across today's economic landscape.

To be honest, today's political and economic context leaves few alternative avenues for development. With the exception of a handful of very large countries—countries that might be able to pursue closed-economy approaches to economic development because of their very size—more trade (broadly understood) is the only game in town.   Poor states today cannot depend on the largess of a sponsoring superpower, or hope for more Official Development Assistance (ODA). Both sources of external support are declining, and will likely dwindle further in the foreseeable future. In short, it is difficult to imagine any alternative route to economic development.   In this context, students of development often ponder how today's developing states can engage world markets in a way that allows them economic growth and democratic accountability. In this pondering, perhaps, the Norwegian experience might provide some lessons.

The period before the First World War was a remarkable, and a remarkably difficult, time in which to live. Norwegians managed to use this period of global markets to climb out of their dependent relationship with Denmark and Sweden (in both economic and political realms) and to secure itself a piece of the growing economic pie. At the same time, like many of its European neighbors, Norway secured a political transformation that brought universal suffrage and a long list of rights and guarantees for the average Norwegian citizen. In the rhetoric of today's globalization debates, we might recognize that this expanding list of democratic rights and worker benefits could have undermined Norway's international competitiveness. Still, for whatever reason, Norway was then willing and able to strike its own precarious balance between justice and efficiency. Norway managed this balancing act while engaging and exploiting international markets and, increasingly, by using political instruments to steer developments in a way that could encourage even greater economic and political development.

This was the initial lesson that I had hoped to impart by describing early Norwegian economic history. The Norwegian example showcases the possibility and hope that economic globalization need not result in growing income divergence across and within countries, or come at the expense of democratic progress and workers' rights. Norway engaged world markets, expanded political voice for the masses, and pulled itself up out of poverty—all in a context that we would today call globalization. It would seem that Norway managed to have its cake and eat it too.

But when all is said and done, I have come to the conclusion that the Norwegian example tells us less about what is possible today, and more about the significant differences that separate our own era of globalization from the one described in the pages above. On the surface, the economic terrain looks remarkably familiar, on several horizons. Most significantly, the development of new technologies has effectively shrunk the globe to its inhabitants, and (as a consequence) created a market that is increasingly global in scope and nature. It is for this reason that today's level of world trade and investment is remarkably similar to the levels enjoyed by countries at the turn of the last century.

The most important lesson to draw from the Norwegian example concerns the differences that separate Norway's opportunities one hundred years ago from those available to developing states today. The most obvious and important difference is the scope and role of international labor migration. Poor states today simply cannot send their excess labor abroad. By limiting the emigration option, we make it more difficult for developing countries today to experience the sort of radical economic catch-up that we saw in the Norwegian example. By limiting the possibility of exit, today's international context limits the political influence of workers at the expense of owners of more mobile assets (such as capital). Simply put: capital owners tend to enjoy freedom of movement abroad; workers do not. This, it would seem, is one of the main reasons that today's states do not appear to feel the same pressure to tame the excesses of globalization (as they did before World War I). Today—in the absence of any threat to massive outward migration, or, for that matter, the threat of a socialist revolution—states find it easier to ignore democratic concerns.

Contemporary economists and policy-makers alike have fooled themselves into thinking that increased trade and capital mobility can be used to substitute for today's lack of international labor mobility. This slight-of-hand has been used to justify the creation of even higher barriers to entry for immigrants from the developing world. But the history of 19th century globalization, and the Norwegian experience, argues otherwise. International labor migration was one of the most important factors behind the real wage and productivity convergence that we saw in the Atlantic economy before World War I. In complex and complementary ways, international migration worked together with international capital mobility and the goods/services trades to produce records of remarkable economic catch-up for some of Europe's poorest states. Today's truncated form of globalization, by relying heavily on trade and investment—at the expense of labor migration—has not been able to deliver the same sort, or scope, of benefits for residents of the world's poorest countries.

In the end, this insensitivity to people's concerns about world markets will likely produce a backlash to today's liberal program (witness, for example, the 'Battle in Seattle'). Free trade, broadly understood, has the potential to produce great winners—as well as great losers. In order to maintain support for free trade over the long haul, states need to be aware of potential winners and losers, and help those who will lose by supporting them as they adjust to new environments. After all, many of today's welfare programs have their antecedents in an earlier period of global market integration: pension programs; unemployment benefits programs; labor market regulations—all of these public policy programs helped countries maintain support for open markets and freer trade. This is one of the most important lessons learned from 19th century globalization. Unfortunately, it is a lesson that is mostly lost on many of today's policy-makers.

Today's global markets are also different in that they are supported by important supranational institutions (such as the World Bank and the International Monetary Fund) that increasingly (if often unwittingly) limited the opportunities available to today's developing states. Although these institutions can provide aid and assistance to poor states in trouble, this assistance usually comes at the price of economic conformity. Worse, international markets increasingly rely on these institutions to provide short-hand information about a state's willingness to embrace liberal markets (this, as a surrogate indicator for a nation's likely development, and/or the risk of default, even appropriation). The result is that poor states (and poor firms in these states) find it difficult to borrow money in international markets if they do not impose a number of market reforms.

The International Monetary Fund was actually established in the wake of World War Two to provide the sort of international financial stability that encouraged economic growth during the gold standard era. As such, it was fairly successful in meeting the needs of developed countries in the period prior to 1971. Today, however, the threat of global financial instability hangs heavily over developing markets. Without wishing to return to an international gold standard, it is important to realize how financial instability today threatens to jeopardize further development in the world's poorest states. This too is a significant difference from the pre World War I period.

Looking back, it is difficult to see how states in today's global context could exploit modern versions of the Norwegian concession laws (although the experiences of the Asian Newly Industrialized Countries (NICs) provide an interesting comparative vantage point). These laws represented the core regulatory instrument in Norway's industrial development, and were absolutely instrumental in establishing the Norwegian petroleum industry as late as the 1970s. Increasingly, however, the developed world's emphasis on an internationally-level playing field, and equal access (regardless of nationality), make it increasingly difficult for states to pursue the sort of policies that can make open markets viable in democratic contexts. Remarkably, Norway—like other developed states— seems to have forgotten its own history and the role that infant industry protection played in it. In international trade venues, Norway increasingly advocates a hands-off, more liberal, approach to economic development in the world's poorest countries.

In the name of free trade, rich countries are imposing new regulations which limit the capacity of poor states to develop themselves. As I have suggested above, the Norwegian example is filled with instances where industrial mimicry (dare I say copyright or patent piracy?) led to substantial learning and subsequent development in Norway. In the 19th century's liberal markets, developing states still had the freedom to flout the patent laws of other countries. Indeed, the Norwegian example suggests that this was a very important means for learning and applying new technologies to the domestic context. This learning opportunity is increasingly difficult in a world trading environment where TRIPS (Trade-Related aspects of Intellectual Property Rights) and TRIMS (Trade-Related Investment Measures) litter the regulatory landscape.

Thus, the lessons we learn from the Norwegian experience are two-fold. On the one hand, Norway's pre World War I economic history helps us understand the realm of the possible. There is no inherent reason for why international trade, foreign direct investment and international migration cannot be used by poor countries to facilitate economic and political (even democratic) development. While no country's experience can be truly replicated or exploited by countries that wish to follow her example, the Norwegian economic example can teach us about the possibilities that exist on a number of different planes. Among these are the ways in which globalization need not be antithetical to economic growth and democratization in the world's poorest countries; how history is filled with examples where states intervened in what were thought of as liberal markets; and where the promise of economic growth may lie in something as simple as learning how to mimic a successful producer.

On the other hand, the Norwegian example teaches us about how different today's international context is from the one that Norway and many other (now developed) states faced one hundred years ago. This does not mean that economic and political development is impossible in this new and different context. It only means that developing countries will have great difficulty in following Norway's earlier path to prosperity. This is, perhaps, the most important lesson, as it helps us to reflect on how the international context might be changed in ways that can help today's poorest countries make their own Cinderella stories come true.

Chapter 9

Interwar Epilogue

The First World War brought the end of an era. The war offers a useful temporal marker for distinguishing between the radically different regime types—both nationally and internationally—that we find before World War I and after World War II. Thus, following Karl Polanyi (1944) and Gerard Ruggie (1982), we tend to think of the period before World War I in terms of unbridled liberalism, and the period after World War II in terms of bridled or embedded liberalism.

Traditionally, the interwar period is seen as a bridge between these two regimes. The severe economic crises that scarred this period can be understood as an explanation for both the fall of the first regime and the rise of the second. It is during this period that new social bargains (for example, the New Deal, social democracy, the social market economy, and so on) were conceived and struck to address the period's economic woes. Although the content of these bargains varied from country to country, most of the developed world came to accept open markets *and* the need to share in the social costs of adjustment that open markets inevitably produce. As we shall see, the interwar economic climate provided fertile ideological and material ground for 'embedding' liberalism.

While this sort of conceptual typology is common and useful, it is always imposed or forced on the data. After all, the past imprints itself on the future, undermining any attempt at simple and clean chronological categories. Thus, as I have endeavored to show in the present book, many of the institutional and ideological roots of the interwar period can be traced to the two decades before World War I, when the need to impose constraints on unfettered markets was first felt.

It is for this reason that I wish to end this book with a short epilogue chapter on the interwar period. My hope is to provide the reader with a small platform, from which he or she can better see the important developments in Norwegian economic history after the Second World War. More importantly, it is only from the perspective offered by the interwar and postwar periods that we come to recognize the uniqueness of the period before World War I. The interwar rupture helps us to see more clearly how World War I brought an end to the liberal economic era.

In particular, I aim to show how radical changes in the international economy—more precisely, a collapse of the liberal prewar order—necessitated a switch to a more interventionist state in many places, including Norway. While much of the conceptual and organizational legacy of this state can be found in the pre World War I period, the intensity and scale of market intervention and regulation increased phenomenally during this period. It is after World War I that we begin to see the institutional and political coalitions that would come to dominate Norway's economic and political landscape for most of the 20th century. Without such an epilogue chapter, it would be difficult to understand the reason for, and nature of, the postwar compromise that was so successful in engineering greater economic growth in Norway.

Having said this, however, I hasten to note that it is not easy to depict the interwar period in short, simple, or general terms. This is a period rich in drama and filled with economic and political instability. In the interwar period we can find economic growth *and* massive unemployment; attempts to return to the prewar liberal order *and* threats of communist revolution and economic isolationism; the dead weight of old ideas *and* vibrant new political alignments. These sorts of contradictions defy any attempt to paint the period in broad strokes.

With this caveat in mind, I intend to use this chapter to describe developments on three fronts. The first section provides a very broad overview of the complex international environment to show how changes adopted by Norway were not uncommon. Norway had to respond to a world that was increasingly nationalist-oriented and isolationist. The second section describes the nature of the Norwegian economic context at the time. It is the nature of Norway's interwar economic crises that help to explain the rise of new political and institutional coalitions at the end of the period. The third section then traces these political developments.

Global contagion

For many contemporary observers, World War I came as a huge and shocking surprise. Liberal ideology held (indeed, it still holds) that increased economic integration limits the potential for conflict among nations. Indeed, some of the greatest liberal thinkers of the prewar period were actively proselytizing this liberal vision: by encouraging economic integration, Europe could expect a more peaceful future. Already in 1846, Richard Cobden (that great British champion of free trade) used a speech in Manchester to paint his picture of a world united by trade, a world that he himself struggled to create:

> I see in the Free Trade principle that which shall act on the moral world as the principle of gravitation in the universe, - drawing men together, thrusting aside the antagonism of race and creed and language, and uniting us in the bonds of eternal peace (Cobden 1846).

More famously, perhaps, was Norman Angell's popular claim in 1910 — just four years before the outbreak of the First *World* War — about the new nature of international exchange. International exchange, he argued, had made states so dependent upon one another 'that war, even when victorious, can no longer achieve the aims for which people strive' (Angell 1910). While Angell came to win the

Nobel Peace Prize in 1933, war again proved itself an instrument for achieving the aims for which people strived (despite the international engagements that were supposed to tie countries closer together).

In the immediate aftermath of World War I, another threat loomed darkly over the political horizon—but this one could hardly have come as a surprise. Political and economic elites were fully aware of the threat posed by socialist revolution, but the threat became all the more menacing in the face of continued economic crises and in the wake of the Bolshevik Revolution in 1917. A new communist specter came to haunt European politics and markets; this specter helped to convince politicians in nascent democratic states that they needed to respond to rising worker dissatisfaction (or risk losing power, influence, or even their lives).

In the light of liberalism's failures, and under the threat of socialist upheaval, global markets imploded on themselves between the two world wars. Although denizens of the period continued to see technological progress and falling transportation costs, global exchange shrunk in the face of growing nationalism and protectionism. World capital, trade and migration flows fell back to their 1870 levels, and poverty and inequality spread across and within countries once connected by international exchange. Fear of the political and economic consequences of economic contagion led individual states to pursue protectionist polices as a means of shoring up sagging domestic markets (and the unemployment that they caused). To do nothing meant risking the radicalization of domestic labor markets, and the threat of socialist revolution.

In short, if integration and interdependence are the most common catch-phrases to describe the period before World War I, then contagion may be the best phrase to describe the interwar period. Economic calamity spread across and within global capital, trade and labor markets. In response to the contagion, countries began to erect protectionist barriers to global trade, capital, and migration flows in an escalating sequence of tit-for-tat, beggar-thy-neighbor policies that spread rapidly around the world.

World trade volumes collapsed during this period. There are two related parts to this sad story: part of the collapse can be explained by a worldwide depression (in the 1930s); another part is the result of spreading protectionist policies. The latter part can be explained as an almost knee-jerk response to developments elsewhere in the international system. In particular, states responded vigorously to two massive tariff increases in the United States. The first was imposed in the wake of World War I to counter the elimination of the wartime income tax and to help pay down debts accumulated during the war. The second was more clearly protectionist: the infamous Smoot-Hawley tariff of 1930. One by one, states constructed their own elaborate systems of protection in an attempt to cordon off domestic economies from the perceived threat that was emanating abroad

At the same time, there was a real need to respond to rising pressure at home to deal with the threats of unemployment, further economic stagnation, and crisis. A new political climate was developing that was more sympathetic to market control and regulation, and more willing to embrace nationalism and isolationism. In Europe, the tragedy of the war and its aftermath explains much of the change, as does the rise of the socialist threat in the wake of the Russian Revolution. In Russia, where the home economy and polity were still devastated by war and revolution, a real threat of attack from its former allies drove the country into greater economic isolation. Likewise, but for different reasons, the US drifted away from liberal integration. The Smoot-Hawley tariff was just one (perhaps the most obvious) of many manifestations of American isolationism. Finally, in Germany, a bitter defeat and a revenge-filled peace fanned a new spirit of nationalism and, ultimately, the rise of fascism.

Like contagion among trading partners, the rise of protectionist trade policies led to protectionist payments' policies and the collapse of the international financial system. This system, symbolized by the gold standard, melted down under a frenzy of competing devaluations as hot money flows and threatening bank crises transmitted contagion from one country to another. Beginning in central Europe in the late 1920s, a string of bank failures (and the threat of many more) spread quickly to Britain, the US and finally France and the gold bloc.

In the same way, national controls on migrant labor were ratcheted up to protect domestic labor markets. This was a traditional response during periods of war, but these controls were usually dropped in the aftermath of hostilities. Yet as protectionist barriers were raised to isolate domestic capital and goods markets, it was relatively easy (even convenient) to maintain and strengthen the war-time controls on international migration. Thus, the US Immigration Acts of 1921 and 1924 were followed up by other states that imposed their own restrictions. As the United States was the largest destination market for international labor at the time, the effect of its protectionist polices was clearly felt in the growing (and increasingly radicalized) labor supply in countries that once exported their excess labor.

In each of these once international markets, states found themselves under increasing pressure to deal with what was understood to be the inherent excesses of liberal exchange. Most notably, Karl Polanyi (1944) referred to the interwar period and postwar compromise as a cataclysmic response to the utopian endeavor of economic liberalism to set up a self-regulating market system. It is easy to frame the Norwegian response in these terms, but to understand that response, we need to examine the nature of Norway's interwar economy.

Growth and unemployment

As was the case for many states, the Norwegian economic record during the interwar period is filled with apparent contradictions. For example, the whole period can be categorized in terms of aggregate economic growth, yet unemployment reached record levels and remained high throughout much of the period. Even the nature of economic policy seemed to change direction in mid-stream. For example, in the 1920s Norwegian policy seemed to be aimed at restoring the prewar liberal order. Although the political authorities recognized the need for some state involvement (of the sort we saw before World War I), the main focus remained on free trade, and a return to the gold standard at prewar parity levels. In the 1930s, however, state intervention became more pronounced, as the Norwegian response to a disintegrating world economic order was to focus on protection, cartelization, regulation and subsidies. While it is common to date the transition to a more interventionist state regime after 1935, when a significant new political alignment develops, the early roots of these policies are traceable to the prewar period.

We can begin this overview by noting that the aggregate economic picture is remarkably bright. Norway experienced significant, albeit uneven, economic growth over the interwar period. Indeed, from 1920 to 1939, Norwegian GDP grew on average over four per cent per year: from 93,909 to 170,679 million kroner in constant 2000 prices (SSB 1994). In only three of these years (1920, 1923, and 1930) did GDP actually fall, and when it did, the fall was brief: just a single year in each case. The same general trend can be found in the period's per capita GDP rate.

Part of this economic expansion can be explained by the liberation of pent-up demand with the end of the war. Norwegians were ready to purchase an astonishing array of new consumer goods and replenish supplies that had dwindled during the war. In the immediate aftermath of the war, one could sense a new optimism that buoyed consumption—at least until a postwar recession hit Europe at the end of 1920. In the aftermath of this recession, and the general depression that followed a decade later, the Norwegian authorities felt that they needed to erect trade barriers to protect the domestic economy from contagion.

Like most countries as the time, Norway sought the solution to its problems in protectionism. Much of Norway's new demand could be satisfied by domestic producers, and this was encouraged with a two-pronged strategy: 1) the state introduced an increasingly protectionist tariff policy; and 2) the government and civil society stoked the growing flames of economic nationalism (for example, by encouraging a 'buy Norwegian' movement). Of course, Norway's small size and openness made it necessary for her to avoid any serious trade conflicts. As a consequence, Norway was generally reluctant to erect protectionist barriers that were as high as the major powers'. Thus, Norwegian tariff increases in the 1930s were significant, but small by international standards: the total level of tariff protection rose from about 10 to 15 per cent.

As evidence of Norway's awareness of the need to encourage multilateral solutions in the face of increasing protectionist pressure, we might briefly note the 1930 establishment of the Oslo Convention. On the initiative of Norway's prime minister at the time, Johan Ludwig Mowinckel, a number of small European states (Denmark, Norway, Sweden, Finland, Belgium, Luxembourg and the Netherlands) came together in what became known as the Oslo Group. Their aim was to encourage a common policy as a neutral bloc for the lowering of trade barriers, the abolition of exchange restrictions and the revival of international credit. Although the convention was renewed in 1937, deteriorating world conditions led the Oslo Group to abandon it in May of 1938.

While the deteriorating international economic climate encouraged greater domestic production of important consumer goods, it also made it more difficult for Norway to specialize in the sort of raw materials-based export niches in which she had excelled before the war.   Foreign markets for these goods shrunk precipitously.   As a consequence, Norwegian industrial exports fell: in 1930, Norway was still exporting about 60 per cent of her industrial production, but in 1939, it had fallen to just over 40 per cent.   Another indicator of the Norwegian costs to international protectionism is evident in the size of her exports and imports, relative to GDP.   In 1914, Norwegian exports represented 35.2 per cent, and imports represented 36.2 per cent, of GDP.   By 1939, however, these shares had sunk to 28.2 and 27.8 per cent respectively (Bergh et al. 1983: 236, appendix table 2).

As we shall see below, Norway's situation was exacerbated by the Bank of Norway's decision to fix the Norwegian krone at its prewar value (parity) in gold.   Since its actual value had sunk by about 50 per cent, this policy sent prices tumbling.   Borrowers found it increasingly difficult to pay back their debts, and countless tragedies took place when businesses, homes, and farms were placed on the auction block.   Workers were forced to accept sizable (nominal) wage cuts,[1] as unemployment and labor conflicts spread across the country.

Indeed, from the workers' perspective, the interwar period can be characterized in terms of one long crisis.   Before the war, between 1905 and 1920, unemployment among union members never rose higher than five per cent.   After 1920, unemployment skyrocketed: from two per cent in 1920 to 17 per cent in 1921 and 1922!   In short, almost one in five trade unionists was unemployed, draining the state-sponsored unemployment scheme in just a few years.   Worse, the union unemployment rate stayed at double-digit numbers, averaging around 15 per cent, throughout the interwar period, with the exception of a single year (1924).   In 1933, one in three trade unionists was out of work and total unemployment is generally estimated to have been in excess of 100,000 (SSB 1968, and Danielsen and Hovland 1995: 326).

These exasperating circumstances sharpened the conflict of interests between labor and capital, producing a significant (and costly) rise in the number of working-days lost to labor conflicts of various types.   Between 1919 and 1939, there were six years when the number of man-days lost to labor conflicts exceeded one million (1921, 1924, 1926, 1927, 1931 and 1937).   In the worst year, 1931, as many as 7,585,832 man-days may have been lost (Hodne 1981: 468).

Thus, Norway's interwar economy can be characterized by fairly constant growth in the aggregate economy as well as by strong indicators of economic crisis (such as tumbling prices, skyrocketing unemployment and a significant number of

---

[1] Because of the radical drop in domestic prices, the real wages of workers may have actually increased slightly during the period.   For example, a union worker in the manufacturing industries was paid about two kroner an hour in 1920, while he received less than 1.4 kroner in 1939 (in other words, a wage drop of about 33 per cent).   Over the same period, however, general prices fell by about 40 per cent.

costly labor conflicts). The explanation for these apparently contradictory observations might lie in the fact that much of Norway's economic growth occurred in a very few export-oriented, and capital-intensive sectors (especially shipping, whaling and the energy-intensive sectors). The remainder of the economy was simply trying to keep its head above water.

As in the period immediately prior to World War I, the Norwegian state was under pressure to improve the nation's investment and employment climate. Generally, we can divide the state's responses to these pressures in three: monetary policy, fiscal policy, and increasing reliance on interest organizations to regulate and control production (and sales).

The interwar period is probably best remembered for the remarkable failures of Norway's central bank. The responsibility for many of this period's hardships can be placed squarely at the feet of its new managing director, Nicolai Rygg. Previously a professor of economics, Rygg took over the bank in the fall of 1920. At about the same time, the Storting had passed a law that aimed to bring the activities of the central bank back to what were considered normal (after the war): note circulation was to be reduced and the currency re-tied to its gold footing. Although the actual rate of linkage to gold was left undecided by the Storting, the central bank—under Rygg's management (with, I should add, the implicit support of the Storting)—aimed for Norway's old (prewar) parity value.

The result was a deflationary crunch that cast thousands of people out of work, caused numerous bankruptcies, crushed Norway's industrial investment and growth potential, and made it more difficult for domestic industries to compete with imported consumer goods. Despite an economic up-turn in the international economy, Norway went through a very serious economic crisis, where the unemployment problem was especially pronounced. This, in turn, led to a long-term debt crisis which hit the agricultural and public sectors particularly hard.

For seven years, Norges Bank tried to squeeze Norwegian prices back into their prewar bounds. In May of 1928, Rygg finally succeeded. His victory, however, proved to be short and illusory, as Norges Bank was again forced to abandon this linkage in 1931.

By 1931, the Norwegian authorities had given up on their deflationary crusade. Following the British example, Norway linked to gold at a devalued rate. Over time, this policy was supported with increased fiscal activism. Together, the effect of this radical policy reversal was a significant increase in domestic demand—spurring home production and slicing the unemployment level. At the same time, the devaluation helped to improve Norway's terms of trade abroad—it made Norwegian goods more affordable there (and at home, as the domestic price of imports rose). It was a policy mix that Norway came to exploit often in the postwar period, especially after 1971 (see Moses 1995 and 2000).

As originally designed, the central bank's policies had delivered a sharp fall in prices and demand. Predictably, the results of this deflationary monetary policy hit workers and farmers particularly hard.[2] This crisis, in turn, seemed to have facilitated cooperation between the Agrarian Party [*Bondepartiet*] and the Labor Party. This new cooperation produced a political coalition, from which much of Norway's postwar economic and political consensus springs.

The first fruit of this new coalition was a minority Labor government, under the leadership of Johan Nygaardsvold, with the support of the Agrarian Party. In May of 1935, this government launched a more aggressively expansionary policy under the Labor Party's 1933 campaign slogan "work for all". The government substantially increased funding for the crisis package that had been launched by the previous Liberal (Mowinckel) government: an increase of some 30 million kroner, from 43 to 76 million kroner, mostly in the form of price supports and new public works. Although this injection was less than what the Labor Party had earlier campaigned for, and Labor was obliged to satisfy a number of demands by the Agrarian Party about earmarking funds for peasants, the policy had a rapid and positive effect on employment levels. More surprisingly, due to an improving home economy and the introduction of a new sales tax, the new policies did not produce a budget deficit: expanding government expenditures were being met by rising state revenues.

Better yet, the government's new fiscal policies were able to piggyback on the central bank's newly expansionary monetary policy (after 1931). As a consequence, interest rates fell to levels that were substantially lower than in the 1920s, working wonders for the country's long-term debt problem.

Finally, the state was increasingly active in encouraging producer organizations in a number of important sectors to regulate production and sales. Given the precarious position of the agricultural sector, we might look briefly at developments there.

Before the war, Norwegian agriculture's response to economic crisis was classically liberal in form: an emphasis was placed on introducing more productive techniques and machinery, and moving into sectors that could best exploit the country's comparative advantage. The response to the interwar crisis was very different, as farmers exploited their organized influence to regulate market conditions with an eye at maintaining prices and production structures.

The most profitable new agricultural niche in Norway had been milk production, and this niche was now hit hardest by the interwar crisis. Between 1920 and 1931, the price of milk fell faster and farther than prices generally. The first response of dairy farmers was to produce more, and this—of course—only drove milk prices further down. Recognizing their mistake, farmers built a national cooperative framework, and secured for it new regulatory powers.

As we have already seen in several previous chapters, the organizational foundation for this cooperative movement had been established in the last two

---

[2] Of course, these groups were not alone. Many businesses went bankrupt, and (as a consequence) the Norwegian banking sector suffered a very serious crisis. Many banks went under, and others needed to be administered by the state. The state's active involvement in rescuing the banking sector meant that it also accrued large debts, which limited its activities in other areas.

decades of the 19th century. But these organizations were given new life in the interwar period, and their influence was fortified with legal support. In 1928, a Norwegian Dairy Exporters Group [*Norske Meieriers Eksportlag*] was established to stabilize the domestic supply of dairy products (by controlling the export of cheese and butter). Then, a regional dairy system was established in 1929 to control the volume of milk going to either consumption or cheese/butter production. This had the effect of controlling the price of milk across different markets. Finally, farmers' organizations were given a majority of seats in a sales council [*omsetningråd*] that was established by a 1930 law to govern milk, egg and pork production. These organizations also secured taxing authority, which allowed them yet another tool for controlling the price difference between consumption and production milk. Finally, the government forced margarine producers to mix butter with margarine—securing a new and larger market for butter producers. As a result of these activities, the price of milk rose throughout the 1930s, securing much needed funds for desperate farmers.

Similar cooperative arrangements can be found in other sectors as well, as producer organizations secured an important and visible role in the institutional landscape. Together, these new institutional arrangements, an increasingly interventionist state (based on a new political coalition of farmers and workers), and a central bank that was willing to break radically with tradition, created a new economic climate in Norway. Jobs, economic growth and a new sense of cooperation and optimism came to characterize the Norwegian economy after 1935.

A new consensus

The political landscape of the interwar period is marked by three inter-related developments. First, we see the slow decline in power of Norway's traditional elites, as the dominance of the Liberal Party is eclipsed first by the Conservative Party, then by a growing labor movement. Second, we see the remarkable transformation of the Labor Party, from revolutionary member of the Comintern to a responsible (and middle-of-the-road) party of government. Finally, we see the birth of a new political coalition between farmers and workers that produces an atmosphere of cooperation and regulation across several sectors.

It is possible (if perhaps a bit too simple) to attribute the decline of traditional elite parties and the rise of Labor in terms of the failed economic polices in the first years after the war. In the early interwar period, the Conservative Party came to eclipse the Liberals as the largest party: three times they formed a government between 1920 and 1928. This was, in part, the result of a new fragmentation of the Norwegian party system, as several new parties joined the political fray. The Agrarian Party was established in 1920, Norway's Communist Party was formed in 1923, and later (in 1933) the Christian People's Party came into being.

As the party in government, voters came to blame the Conservatives for the dismal economic record of the time. Thus, the postwar depression and financial crises, the growing debt problem, and (especially) the bull-headed commitment to return to prewar gold parity, led directly to the rise of the first Labor (Hornsrud) government in 1927. Although this government sat for just eighteen days, it represents an important turning point in Norwegian politics. A new, more moderate Labor Party was now poised to play a significant role in Norwegian political life.

But in describing this new role for the Norwegian labor movement it is important not to exaggerate the differences that separated the bourgeois and socialist parties in parliament. There was a broad consensus—that stretched across the political spectrum—for a more interventionist state and new social policies. The biggest difference between the two blocs may have been over their willingness to borrow money to pay for new programs at a time where the government was already saddled with a significant amount of debt. At the time, the Labor Party was able to recognize the seriousness of the crisis and was willing to borrow money to address the problem.

The rise of the new Labor Party (DNA) is a story in itself. In Chapter 3 we briefly touched on the growing radicalism of the Norwegian labor movement before World War I. In the wake of the Bolshevik Revolution, the radical Tranmæl faction took over the DNA in 1918, when the Party's National Congress voted it into the Third International. Indeed, a resolution at this conference reserved the right for the party to lead a revolution of the masses, even if it did not secure a majority in the Storting. In 1921, at another Labor Party Congress, the party adopted the so-called 21 'Moscow theses' (binding the Party to Comintern decisions).

Labor Party radicalism was fed by an increasingly hostile industrial environment between workers and employers. After the postwar (World War I) recession, the nation's first arbitration law had lapsed, and strike and lock-out activity increased significantly. When a lock-out offensive started in 1921, the LO responded with a national strike, utilizing more than 150,000 workers. The result was a disaster for labor: prices and demand were so low that employers had little to lose by firing their workers. As a result, LO membership dive-bombed, from 142,000 in 1920, to about 84,000 in 1922. A new arbitration law in 1922 helped calm the situation, and political strikes became less important. But the years between 1920 and 1935 mark a low point in Norwegian industrial relations as 24,448,000 man-days were lost to disputes during this time (as compared to only 5,002,000 days for the 1905-1920 period) (Galenson 1952: 141).

The 1920s were a remarkably tumultuous period for the Norwegian Labor Party. In 1921, a growing faction officially withdrew from the party and constituted themselves as Norway's Social Democratic Labor Party. Two years later, in 1923, the party again split—this time to the left. Then, when a majority of the DNA (with Tranmæl as leader) finally decided to leave the Comintern, a small opposition group left the DNA to form the Norwegian Communist Party, along strictly Leninist lines.

By 1927 the social democratic wing of the Party had returned to the fold, and the new Labor Party was able to win 59 of the 150 seats in parliament (compared to 32 seats, just three years earlier). While 59 seats were not enough to maintain power for the rest of the decade, it signaled the beginning of a new cleavage in Norwegian politics. After 1927, we can begin to see the old Conservative-Liberal cleavage being replaced by a more significant cleavage between socialist and non-socialist (bourgeois[3]) blocs.

This new cleavage was particularly evident in the 1930 election campaign, when impressive campaigning by the non-socialist bloc managed to turn back a growing socialist movement. As a consequence, the Labor Party lost 12 of its 59 seats in parliament, while the Conservatives gained 13 seats (from 31 to 44). But the 1933 election was the last significant electoral victory for the bourgeois parties. The underlying political tide was shifting, bringing with it the third significant development of the interwar period: the establishment of a new class compromise between labor and peasants, in opposition to the interests of employers and Norway's traditional elites.

By the time that the effects of the 1929 New York stock market crash were added to a growing list of economic woes, the Norwegian electorate was growing tired of the ineffectiveness of Conservative and Liberal solutions. Both parties (but especially the Liberals) argued that the state's precarious financial situation precluded any possibility of greater state intervention in the economy. To the electorate, the non-socialist bloc was increasingly seen as uncaring and ineffective—offering nothing but more of the same, unpopular, policy responses. The public was in search of more radical solutions and supported greater economic intervention in the form of subsidies and supports. At the same time, the Labor Party was becoming more acceptable to most voters, as it had managed to distance itself from its revolutionary past and present a more moderate, democratic and nationalist image to the electorate.

This is the political and economic context that produced the new crisis compromise [*kriseforliket*] of 1935. There was now broad political support for more government intervention in the economy, more regulation and control of the marketplace to protect the interest of workers and peasants, and new social reforms aimed at helping society's most needy. At the same time, a 1935 Main Agreement between the LO and NAF provided a more amiable economic environment, and Norwegian labor relations were increasingly characterized by moderation.

On the social policy front, a number of earlier policies were strengthened and expanded. The 1909 sickness insurance plan was extended to cover new groups, the law on worker protection was revisited and expanded to cover new categories of workers, and a law providing benefits for the disabled was introduced in 1936. While the Storting had voted to provide unemployment insurance for all Norwegians in 1923, economic difficulties had prevented its implementation until

---

[3] In the Scandinavian context, non-socialist parties are commonly (and traditionally) referred to as 'bourgeois'. The term, as employed here, is not meant to be derogatory, or as a signal of any underlying ideological commitment on the part of the author.

1938. Finally, after decades of disagreement, an old-age pension scheme was introduced in 1936. Thus, by the time that World War II arrived unannounced on Norway's shores, the country was already a world leader in the area of social policy.

                                        *

This point is as good as any, on which to end our story. We find ourselves now in a position to better understand the political and institutional context that would come to dominate Norwegian economic policy in the postwar (World War II) period. A new political constellation, representing a broad alliance of workers and peasants, came to dominate the political landscape, creating the ideological, political and institutional context that would deliver postwar economic growth.

I hope that this epilogue chapter has helped us reflect on how far the Norwegian economy had come since 1865. From the perspective of the interwar period it is easier to see the uniqueness of the period prior to World War I, when the Norwegian economy had its first serious engagement with more liberal, and global, markets. But from this perspective we also see how many of the ideological, political and institutional components of the interwar compromise can be traced to the period before the war.

The interwar and postwar periods are characterized by increased state involvement in economic exchange: by the government's willingness to embed market exchange in institutions that are responsive to democratic influences. In doing so, this new compromise was able to legitimate and extend support for the sort of global exchange upon which Norway—as a small country—depends.

This new political climate was a reaction to the perceived injustices of an earlier, unbridled, liberal order. This dissatisfaction with the liberal order was already evident before the outbreak of World War I. I have endeavored to show this in many of the preceding chapters. Unfortunately, it took two world wars before the developed world finally came to grips with the need to tame the excesses of liberal markets with political controls. It is my hope that this lesson will not be lost on tomorrow's political and economic elites.

Bibliography

Angell, Norman (1910), *The Great Illusion*, New York and London, author synopsis on the Internet at http://www.lib.byu.edu/~rdh/wwi/1914m/illusion.html, accessed 20 September 2004.

Bairoch, P. (1989), 'European Trade Policy, 1815-1914', in P. Mathias and S. Pollard (eds), *The Cambridge Economic History of Europe*, Vol. III, Cambridge University Press, Cambridge.

Bairoch, P. (1993), *Economics and World History: Myths and Paradoxes*, Wheatsheaf, Brighton.

Berend, I. and G. Ranki (1982), *The European Periphery and Industrialization 1780-1914*, Cambridge University Press, Cambridge.

Bergh, Trond, Tore Hanisch, Even Lange and Helge Pharo (1983), *Norge fra u-land til i-land*, Gyldendal, Oslo.

Blegen, Theodore C. (1931), *Norwegian Migration to America, 1825-1860*, The Norwegian-American Historical Association, Northfield, Minnesota.

Borjas, George J. (1990), *Friends or Strangers: The Impact of Immigration on the US Economy*, Basic Books, New York.

Brautaset, Camilla (2001), 'The emergence of an independent Norwegian economic policy', in Michalis Psalidopoulos (ed), *Economic Thought and Policy in Less Developed Europe: 19th Century*, Routledge, Florence, KY, pp. 37-54.

Carr, E. H. ([1961] 1990), *What is History?*, Penguin, London.

Castles, Stephen and Mark J. Miller (1993), *The Age of Migration*, The Guilford Press, New York.

Christophersen, H. O. (1962), *Eilert Sundt. En dikter i kjensgjerninger*, Gyldendal, Oslo.

Cobden, Richard (1846) 'Free Trade with All Nations', A speech delivered in Manchester England, 15 January 1846, accessed on 1 September 2004 from the Internet at <http://www.cooperativeindividualism.org/cobdenonfreetrade.html>.

Danielsen, Rolf and Edgar Hovland (1995), 'The inter-war years', in Danielsen et al., *Norway: A History from the Vikings to Our Own Times*, Scandinavian University Press, Oslo, pp. 314-333.

Derry, T. K. (1973), *A History of Modern Norway 1814-1972*, Clarendon, Oxford.

Edelstein, Michael (1994). 'Foreign Investment and Accumulation, 1860-1914', in Roderick Floud and D. McCloskey, eds., *The Economic History of Britain Since 1700*, 2nd ed., Vol. 2, Cambridge University Press, Cambridge.

Encyclopedia Britannica (1911), 'Railways', accessed on 30 July 2004 from the Internet at <http://38.1911encyclopedia.org/R/RA/RAILWAYS.htm>.

Faini, Riccardo (2005), 'Migration, Remittances, and Growth', forthcoming in George J. Borjas and Jeffery Crisp (eds), *Poverty, International Migration and Asylum*, Palgrave, Basingstoke, Chapter 8.

Finansdepartementet (1842), *NOS Beretning om Kongeriket Norges Oeconomiske Tilstand 1836-40*. Finans Handels og Tolddepartementets underdanigste Foredrag 9.11.1842, Oslo.

Fuglum, Per (1978), *Norge i støpeskjeen 1884-1919*, Vol. 12 in *Cappelens Norgeshistorie*, Cappelen, Oslo.

Galenson, Walter (1952), 'Scandinavia', in Walter Galenson (ed), *Comparative Labor Movements*, Prentice Hall, New York.

Gallup, John Luke and Jeffrey D. Sachs (1999), 'Geography and Economic Development', CAER II Discussion Paper No. 39, Harvard Institute for International Development (March), accessed on 10 August 2004 from the Internet at <http://www.cid.harvard.edu/caer2/htm/content/papers/paper39/paper39.pdf>.

Gourevitch, Peter (1978), 'The Second Image Reversed: The International Sources of Domestic Politics', *International Organization* 32 (Autumn), pp. 881-911.

Hamilton, Alexander (1791), *Report on the Subject of Manufactures*, accessed on 27 September 2004 from the Internet at <http://www.coinfacts.com/mint_history/mint_history_1781_1791/alexander_hamilton_report_1791_page1.htm>.

Hatton, Timothy J. and Jeffrey G. Williamson (1998), *The Age of Mass Migration. Causes and Economic Impact*, Oxford University Press, New York.

Heilbroner, Robert L. (1985), *The Making of Economic Society*, seventh edition, Prentice-Hall, Englewood Cliffs, NJ.

Hodne, Fritz (1973), 'Growth in a Dual Economy—The Norwegian Experience 1814-1914', *Economy and History*, Vol. XVI, pp. 81-110, reprinted in Karl Gunnar Persson (eds) (1993), *The Economic Development of Denmark and Norway since 1870*, Edward Elgar, Aldershot England, pp.45-74.

Hodne, Fritz (1981), *Norges økonomiske historie 1815-1970*, J. W. Cappelens, Oslo.

Hodne, Fritz and Ola Honningdal Grytten (1992), *Norsk Økonomi 1900-1990*, TANO, Oslo.

Hodne, Fritz and Ola Honningdal Grytten (2000), *Norsk Økonomi i det 19. århundre*, Fagbokforlaget, Bergen.

Holt, W., Strömme Svendsen, A., Wasberg, G. (1963), 'Industriens gjennombrudd', in Johan T. Ruud (et al.) (eds), *Dette er Norge 1814-1964*, Vol. 2, Gyldendal, Oslo.

Hovde, B. J. (1934), 'Notes on the Effects of Emigration upon Scandinavia', *The Journal of Modern History*, Vol. 6 (3), pp. 253-279.

Hovland, Edgar (1995), 'Modern Norway takes shape, 1875-1920', in Rolf Danielsen, Ståle Dyrvik, Tore Grønlie, Knut Helle and Edgar Hovland's *Norway: A History from the Vikings to Our Own Times*, Scandinavian University Press, Oslo, pp. 271-296.

Hovland, Edgar and Helge Wallum Nordvik (1997), 'Det industrielle gjennombrudd i Norge 1840-1914 med samtidens og ettertidens øyne', in Bjørn L. Basberg, Helge W. Nordvik and Gudmund Stang (eds), *I det lange løp. Essays i økonomisk historie tilegnet Fritz Hodne*, Fagbokforlaget, Bergen, pp. 61-85.

Hvidt, Kristian (1975), *Flight to America: The Social Background of 300,000 Danish Emigrants*, Academic Press, New York.

Iregui, Ana María (2005), 'Efficiency Gains from the Elimination of Global Restrictions on Labour Mobility: An Analysis using a Multiregional CGE Model', in George J. Borjas and Jeffery Crisp (eds), *Poverty, International Migration and Asylum*, Palgrave, Basingstoke, Chapter 10.

Jago, Lucy (2001), *The Northern Lights. The True Story of the Man who Unlocked the Secrets of the Aurora Borealis*, Alfred Knopf, New York.

Johnson, Harry G. (1967), *Economic Policies toward Less Developed Countries*, Praeger, New York.

Jæger, Oskar (1930), *Finanslære*, Aschehoug, Oslo.

Jörberg, Lennard (1970), *The Fontana Economic History of Europe. The Industrial Revolution in Scandinavia 1850-1914*, Volume 4, Fontana, London, Chapter 8.

Jörberg, Lennard (1973), 'The Industrial Revolution in the Nordic Countries', in Carlo M. Cipolla (ed), *The Fontana Economic History of Europe*, Vol. 4 (2), Collins/Fontana Books, London, pp. 375-485.

Katzenstein, Peter (1985), *Small States in World Markets*, Cornell University Press, Ithaca.

Keynes, J. M. (1919), *The Economic Consequences of the Peace*. Available online at <http://socserv2.socsci.mcmaster.ca/~econ/ugcm/3ll3/keynes/peace.htm>, accessed 27. September 2004.

Kindleberger, Charles P. (1951), 'Group Behavior and International Trade', *The Journal of Political Economy*, Vol. 59 (1), pp. 30-46.

Kindleberger, Charles P. (1967), *Europe's Postwar Growth: The Role of Labor Supply*, Harvard University Press, Cambridge.

Krasner, Stephen (1976), 'State Power and the Structure of international Trade', *World Politics*, Vol. 28 (3), pp. 317-347.

Lewis, W. Arthur (1954), 'Economic Development with Unlimited Supplies of Labour', *The Manchester School*, Vol. 22(2), pp. 139-91.

Lieberman, Sima (1970), *The Industrialization of Norway 1800-1920*, Universitetsforlaget, Oslo.

List, George Friedrich ([1841] 1856), *National System of Political Economy*, Lippincott, Philadelphia.

Lowenfeld, Henry (1909), *Investment: an Exact Science*, The Financial Review of Reviews, London.

Markusen, J. R. (1983), 'Factor Movements and Commodity Trade as Complements', *Journal of International Economics*, Vol. 14, pp. 341-356.

Moe, Thorvald (1970). 'Some Economic Aspects of Norwegian Population Movements 1740-1940: An Econometric Study', *The Journal of Economic History*, Vol. 30 (1), pp. 267-270.

Moses, Jonathon W. (1995), 'Devalued Priorities: The politics of Nordic exchange rate regimes compared', PhD dissertation filed at the Department of Political Science, University of California, Los Angeles.

Moses, Jonathon W. (2000), *OPEN States in the Global Economy: The Political Economy of Small-State Macroeconomic Management*, Macmillan, Basingstoke.

Moses, Jonathon W. and Bjørn Letnes (2004), 'The Economic Costs to International Labor Restrictions: Revisiting the Empirical Discussion', *World Development*, Vol. 32 (10), pp. 1609-1626.

Moses, Jonathon W. and Bjørn Letnes (2005), 'If People were Money: Estimating the Gains and Scope of Free Migration', forthcoming in George J. Borjas and Jeffery Crisp (eds), *Poverty, International Migration and Asylum*, Palgrave, Basingstoke, Chapter 9.

NationMaster (2004), 'Map & Graph: Health--Life expectancy at birth (total population)', available on the Internet at <http://www.nationmaster.com/red/graph-B/hea_lif_exp_at_bir_tot_pop&int=10>, accessed 5 September 2004.

Nerbøvik, Jostein (1999), *Norsk Historie 1860-1914*, Det Norske Samlaget, Oslo.

New Internationalist (2000), 'Migration: A journey through time', *New Internationalist* website <http://www.oneworld.org/ni/issue305/journey.html>, accessed 12 November 2000.

Norges Bank (2004), 'Historisk Prisindeks', available on the Internet at <http://www.norges-bank.no/front/statistikk/no/historisk_kp/Data!A1>, accessed 8 June 2004.

North, Douglass C. (1990), *Institutions, Institutional Change and Economic Performance*, Cambridge University Press, Cambridge.

OIS [Office of Immigration Statistics] (2003), *2002 Yearbook of Immigration Statistics*, OIS, Washington DC, available on the Internet at: <http://uscis.gov/graphics/shared/aboutus/statistics/Yearbook2002.pdf>, accessed 10 August 2004.

O'Rourke, Kevin Hjortshøj and Jeffrey G. Williamson (1995a), 'Open Economy Forces and Late Nineteenth Century Swedish Catch-Up. A Quantitative Accounting', *Scandinavian Economic History Review*, Vol. XLIII (2), pp. 171-203.

O'Rourke, Kevin Hjortshøj and Jeffrey G. Williamson (1995b), 'Education, Globalization and Catch-Up: Scandinavia in the Swedish Mirror', *Scandinavian Economic History Review*, Vol. XLIII (3), pp. 287-309.

O'Rourke, Kevin Hjortshøj and Jeffrey G. Williamson (1995c), 'Open Economy Forces and Late 19th Century Scandinavian Catch-Up', Harvard Institute of Economic Research, Discussion Paper No. 1709 (January).

O'Rourke, Kevin Hjortshøj and Jeffrey G. Williamson (2000), *Globalization and History*, MIT Press, Cambridge.

Pax (2003), 'Arbeidskonflikter i Norge', *Pax Lexicon* (1978-92), available on the Internet at <http://www.leksikon.org/art.php?n=133>, accessed 12 December 2003.

Polanyi, Karl (1944), *The Great Transformation*, Beacon, Boston.

Potts, Lydia (1990), *The World Labour Market. A History of Migration*, translated by Terry Bond, Zed, London.

Pritchett, Lant (1997), 'Divergence, Big Time', *Journal of Economic Perspectives*, Vol.11 (3), pp. 3-17.

Ricardo, David ([1817] 1965), *The Principles of Political Economy and Taxation*, Dutton, New York.

Riis, Christian and Tore Thonstad (1989), 'A Counterfactual Study of Economic Impacts of Norwegian Emigration and Capital Imports', in I. Gordon & A.P. Thirlwall (eds.), *European Factor Mobility: Trends and Consequences*, Macmillan, Basingstoke, pp. 116-32.

Rostow, W. W. (1960), *The Stages of Economic Growth*, Cambridge University Press, Cambridge.

Ruggie, John (1982), 'International Regimes, Transactions, and Change: Embedded Liberalism in the Postwar International Order', *International Organization*, Vol. 36 (2), pp. 379-415.

Samuelson, Paul A. (1976), *Economics*, tenth edition, McGraw-Hill, New York.

Schmitter, P. and G. Lehmbruch (eds) (1979), *Trends towards Corporatist Intermediation*, Sage, London.

Seip, Jens Arup (1963), *Fra embedsmannsstat til ettpartistat og andre essays*, Universitetsforlaget, Oslo.

Seip, Jens Arup (1974), *Utsikt over Norges historie*, Vol. I, Gyldendal, Oslo.

Seip, Jens Arup (1981), *Utsikt over Norges historie*, Vol. II, Gyldendal, Oslo.

Sejersted, Francis (1984), *Demokrati og rettstat*, Universitetsforlaget, Oslo.

Sejersted, Francis (1993), 'Den norske Sonderweg', in Francis Sejersted, *Demokratisk kapitalisme*, Universitetsforlaget, Oslo, pp. 169-208.

Semmingsen, Ingrid (1980), *Norway to America. A History of the Migration*, translated by Einar Haugen, University of Minnesota Press, Minneapolis.

Skeldon, Ronald (1997), *Migration and Development*, Addison Wesley Longman, Essex.

Slagstad, Rune (1998), *De nasjonale strateger*, Pax, Oslo.

Smith, Adam (1776 [1904]), *An Inquiry into the Nature and Causes of the Wealth of Nations*, fifth edition, Methuen and Co. Ltd, London, available on the Internet at <http://www.econlib.org/library/Smith/smWN1.html>, accessed 27 September 2004.

SSB [Statistisk Sentralbyrå] (1965), *Ekteskap, Fødsler og Vandringer i Norge 1856-1960*, Samfunnsøkonomisk studier nr. 13, SSB, Oslo.

SSB [Statistisk Sentralbyrå] (1966), *Langtidslinjer i Norsk økonomi 1865-1960*, Samfunnsøkonomisk studier nr. 16, authored by Mr. Juul Bjerke, SSB, Oslo.

SSB [Statistisk Sentralbyrå] (1967), *Det Norske Kredittmarked siden 1900*, Samfunnsøkonomisk studier nr. 19, authored by Mr. Hermod Skånland, SSB, Oslo.

SSB [Statistisk Sentralbyrå] (1968), *Historisk Statistikk*, SSB, Oslo.

SSB [Statistisk Sentralbyrå] (1994), *Historisk Statistikk*, SSB, Oslo.

SSB [Statistisk Sentralbyrå] (2000), 'Skatter og avgifter til staten. 1851-1999. Mill. Kr', accessed on 20 September 2004 from the Internet at <http://www.ssb.no/emner/historisk_statistikk/aarbok/ht-1201-637.html>.

SSB [Statistisk Sentralbyrå] (2004) 'Bruttonasjonalprodukt, etter anvendelse. Faste 2000-priser. 1865-2003. Millioner kr', available on the Internet at <http://ssb.no/emner/historisk_statistikk/aarbok/ht-0901-355.html>, accessed 10 September 2004.

Stonehill, Arthur (1965), *Foreign Ownership in Norwegian enterprise*, Samfunnsøkonomisk studier nr. 14, SSB, Oslo.

Taylor, A.M. and J.G. Williamson (1994), 'Convergence in the Age of Mass Migration', NBER Working Paper No. 4711, April, NBER, Cambridge Massachusetts. Accessed on 10 September 2004 from the Internet at <http://www.econ.ucdavis.edu/faculty/amtaylor/papers/w4711.pdf >.

Thomas, Brinley (1961), *International Migration and Economic Development*, UNESCO, Paris.

Tilly, Charles (1978), 'Migration in Modern European History', in William H. McNeill and Ruth S. Adams (eds), *Human Migration. Patterns and Policies*, Indiana University Press, Bloomington, pp. 48-74.

Torpey, John (2000), *The Invention of the Passport*, Cambridge University Press, Cambridge.

Utvandringskomiteen 1912-1913 (1913-15), 'Lov om utvandring, m.v.', Indstilling 11, Christiania [Oslo].

Westergaard, Harald (1926), *Den Økonomiske Udvikling i det Nittende Aarhundrede*, Gyldendalske Boghandel Nordisk Forlag, Copenhagen.

Wicksell, Knut (1882), *Om utvandringen: Dess betydelseoch orsaker*, Albert Bonniers Forlag, Stockholm.

Williamson, Jeffrey G. (1996), 'Globalization and Inequality Then and Now: The Late 19th and Late 20th Centuries Compared', NBER Working paper No. 5491, NBER, Cambridge, Massachusetts.

Winters, L. A. (2002), 'The Economic Implications of Liberalising Mode 4 Trade', paper prepared for the Joint WTO-World Bank Symposium on 'The Movement of Natural Persons (Mode 4) under the GATS', Geneva, 11-12 April, preliminary (8 April) draft accessed on 27 September 2004 from the Internet at <http://www.tessproject.com/guide/pubs/mode4/Economic_Implications_of%2 0Lib_Mode4_Trade.pdf>.

World Bank (2000), *World Development Report 2000/2001: Attacking Poverty*, World Bank, Washington DC.

Øien, Arne (1963), 'Den offentlige husholdning', in Jouhan T. Ruud, Aronld Eskeland, Gunnar Randrs and Magne Skodvin (eds), *Dette er Norge 1814-1964*, Vol. 2, Gyldendal Norsk Forlag, Oslo, pp. 175-198.

Index

For Product Safety Concerns and Information please contact our EU
representative GPSR@taylorandfrancis.com Taylor & Francis Verlag GmbH,
Kaufingerstraße 24, 80331 München, Germany

Printed and bound by CPI Group (UK) Ltd, Croydon, CR0 4YY

01/05/2025

01858390-0001